Careers in Internet Technology

Careers in Internet Technology

Bradley Steffens

ReferencePoint
Press®

About the Author

Bradley Steffens is an award-winning poet, playwright, novelist, and author of more than thirty nonfiction books for children and young adults. He is a two-time recipient of the San Diego Book Award for Best Young Adult and Children's Nonfiction: His *Giants* won the 2005 award, and his *J.K. Rowling* claimed the 2007 prize. Steffens also received the Theodor S. Geisel Award for best book by a San Diego County author in 2007.

© 2017 ReferencePoint Press, Inc.
Printed in the United States

For more information, contact:
ReferencePoint Press, Inc.
PO Box 27779
San Diego, CA 92198
www.ReferencePointPress.com

Picture Credits:
Cover: Phovoir/Shutterstock.com
13: Yuri Arcurs/iStockphoto
20: vgajic/iStockphoto
53: PeopleImages/iStockphoto
62: humonia/iStockphoto

LIBRARY OF CONGRESS CATALOGING-IN-PUBLICATION DATA

Names: Steffens, Bradley, 1955- author.
Title: Careers in Internet technology / by Bradley Steffens.
Description: San Diego, CA : ReferencePoint Press, Inc., 2017. | Series: High-tech careers | Includes bibliographical references and index.
Identifiers: LCCN 2016035291 (print) | LCCN 2016036091 (ebook) | ISBN 9781682821145 (hardback) | ISBN 9781682821152 (eBook)
Subjects: LCSH: Internet--Vocational guidance--Juvenile literature.
Classification: LCC TK5105.875.I57 S7545 2017 (print) | LCC TK5105.875.I57 (ebook) | DDC 621.39/81023--dc23
LC record available at https://lccn.loc.gov/2016035291

Contents

Introduction: A Growing Network of Jobs — 6

User Experience Designer — 10

Web Developer — 18

Search Engine Optimization Manager — 26

Database Administrator — 34

Cybersecurity Analyst — 42

Social Media Specialist — 50

Mobile App Developer — 58

Penetration Tester — 66

Interview with a Search Engine
Optimization Manager — 73

Other Jobs in Internet Technology — 76

Index — 77

A Growing Network of Jobs

With 40 percent of the world's population—about 3.5 billion people —using the Internet, the growth in Internet-related occupations has been staggering. The Bureau of Labor Statistics (BLS), an agency within the US Department of Labor, reports that in the ten-year period from 2004 to 2014, 71 percent of the new jobs in science and engineering were in computing. Currently 3.9 million Americans are employed in the information technology sector, which includes both Internet- and non-Internet-related computing jobs. That figure is expected to grow to 4.4 million jobs by 2024, a growth rate of 12 percent—about double the rate of all occupations. Many Internet-related jobs are expected to grow even faster than that. For example, the BLS forecasts the growth rate of web developer jobs to be 27 percent by 2024 and the growth rate of cybersecurity jobs to be 18 percent.

One of the factors driving the growth in Internet careers is the sheer number of devices being connected to the Internet, including 2.6 billion smartphones already in the hands of Internet users. According to Juniper Research, the total number of devices connected to the Internet, often referred to as the Internet of Things (IoT), now stands at 13.4 billion. Juniper forecasts that number will rise to 38.5 billion devices in 2020, an increase of more than 285 percent. Many of these devices, such as smart televisions and refrigerators, are in the home, but the vast majority of connected devices are in the industrial and public services sectors, including retail, agriculture, smart buildings, and smart grid applications. All of these devices require software applications, or apps, to make them perform their required tasks. They also need to be designed for easy use, networked properly and securely, and have their data stored in secure but easily accessible databases. The IoT will be supported by an army of Internet technology professionals.

The IoT will play an important role in the next stage of Internet usage, often referred to as Web 3.0 or pervasive computing. In this usage model, machines will interact with each other over the Internet, with little or no human involvement, other than creating settings and issuing an occasional command. For example, a person might give an app called an Intelligent Personal Assistant (IPA) his or her preferences for air travel: favorite airlines, seating, and times of day. The user might tell the IPA, "I want to fly to London on February 10, returning on February 24." The IPA would then look at all available flights, make the reservation, pay for the ticket from the user's bank account, send the e-ticket to the user's phone, enter the travel dates into the user's calendar, and even send a reminder to the user ahead of the travel date—all from the user's single command. A great deal of software will have to be developed and large amounts of data will have to be stored and readily retrievable to make pervasive computing possible, creating thousands of new jobs.

A Popular Pastime Generates Jobs

The popularity of social networking is also driving growth of the Internet technology job sector. In 2016, the total number of all social networking users stood at 2.22 billion. The Radicati Group forecasts that number to rise to 2.5 billion by 2019. The growth in social networking has fueled a number of businesses. Many companies have created software programs to analyze the vast amount of data being posted in social media. This data is known as Big Data because of its size, the speed at which it is created, and the varied types of data— text, videos, pictures—it contains. Companies performing Big Data analytics mine the social media posts to find trends that can be used to improve customer relations, attract new customers, and develop new products and services. The processing of Big Data has created tens of thousands of new jobs and is forecast to create even more in the future.

Digital marketing and communications companies also are cashing in on the opportunities presented by social networking. These firms advertise on social networking websites, attempting to acquire customers and increase sales on behalf of their clients. According to

Internet Technology Careers

Occupation	Entry-Level Education	2015 Median Pay
Multimedia Artist and Animator	Bachelor's degree	$63,970
Graphic Designer	Bachelor's degree	$46,900
Web Developer	Associate's degree	$64,970
Software Developer	Bachelor's degree	$100,690
Computer Hardware Engineer	Bachelor's degree	$111,730
Database Administrator	Bachelor's degree	$81,710
Information Security Analyst	Bachelor's degree	$90,120
Computer Support Specialist	Associate's degree	$51,470
Network and Computer Systems Administrator	Bachelor's degree	$77,810
Computer Information and Systems Manager	Bachelor's degree	$131,600
Computer Systems Analyst	Bachelor's degree	$85,800
Computer Programmer	Bachelor's degree	$79,530

Bureau of Labor Statistics, *Occupational Outlook Handbook*. www.bls.gov/ooh.

the CMO Council, a global network of marketing executives, spending on mobile Internet marketing is doubling each year, and two-thirds of the growth in consumer advertising is in digital. Digital marketing, which scarcely existed ten years ago, now employs tens of thousands of people and is expected to employ even more as Internet users spend increasing amounts of time browsing their favorite websites, posting pictures, and messaging friends.

Filling the Skills Gap

Internet-related jobs also pay very well, in part because there is a shortage of people with the skills to perform the new and emerging duties. A 2016 report by the IT staffing company Robert Half Technology found that 60 percent of chief information officers find it somewhat or very challenging to find skilled IT professionals today. The UK Council of Professors and Heads of Computing estimated that Big Data alone has created around 4.4 million jobs globally, but there are only enough skilled people to fill one-third of these positions. In a survey of 760 companies across twenty-nine states in the United States and three Canadian provinces, the nonprofit Technology Councils of North America found 83 percent of employers reported a shortage of software development professionals. As a result of the shortage of qualified candidates, the BLS reported the median annual wage for computer and information technology occupations was $81,430 in May 2015, which was more than double the median annual wage for all occupations. Careers in Internet technology offer a bright future for the technically inclined as well as those who enjoy writing, graphic design, product design, and creating videos—all of which are needed by companies doing business on or for the Internet.

User Experience Designer

A user experience designer, also known as a UX designer, is responsible for planning how all the parts of a product or website combine to create a positive experience for the user. The goal is to engage the user in a memorable way that leaves a lasting impression about the product, brand, or company the website represents. "User Experience Design is the process of development and improvement of quality interaction between a user and all facets of a company," Emil Lamprecht, a counselor with online development company CareerFoundry, writes on the company's blog.

Long before the web designer, also known as the user interface (UI) designer, creates the visual layer of the website, the UX designer imagines how the experience of the website visitor should unfold to create the desired impression. The UX designer bases this concept not only on his or her understanding of the organization's

At a Glance:
User Experience Designer

Minimum Educational Requirements
Bachelor's degree or equivalent

Personal Qualities
Excellent people skills; analytical; able to think and communicate visually

Certification and Licensing
Optional

Working Conditions
Indoors

Salary Range
About $61,000 to $137,000

Number of Jobs
As of 2014 about 100,000

Future Job Outlook
Growth of 18 percent by 2025

product, but also upon research about the needs, desires, and wishes of people who use the product, or, if the product is new, those who might want to use it. "User Experience Design is not a market research job, though it does utilize many of the same techniques to achieve a complex end goal: The structure, analysis and optimization of a customer's experience with a company and its products," writes Lamprecht. The UX designer might work with the marketing department to conduct surveys or interviews with customers or product users to find out what is most important to them.

Based on the research, the UX designer maps out the web visitor's experience by creating a wireframe, a step-by-step plan for how the visitor will navigate the website. "A wireframe—a rough guide for the layout of a website or app—is the deliverable most famously associated with being a UX Designer," writes Matthew Magain, a UX designer in Australia, on the SitePoint blog. The wireframe shows the interactive features of a web page, the navigational path through the website, and the way they work together to create the desired experience.

Wireframes can take several forms, and the UX designer will decide which works best in each situation. A wireframe can be as simple as a series of diagrams drawn with pencil and paper or on a whiteboard. The UX designer will often add notes to describe the interaction between the various elements of a web page and between one page and another. The UX designer also can create a wireframe with software tools that not only capture the designer's thinking but also make it possible to transform the wireframe into an interactive prototype—a working model of the website. The prototype can then be used by the UI designer and the front end developer to build the website the visitor sees. "Wireframing your web page before going to the programming step will ensure that your pages perform effectively on all screens," Rosemary Brisco writes on the website of ToTheWeb, a digital marketing firm where Brisco works as a search visibility expert.

Once a rough version of the website is built, the UX designer will invite volunteers to use the website—a process known as user testing. Usually the designer will ask the users to perform certain tasks, encouraging them to describe the experience of navigating the website as they go. The UX designer will use data from the user testing to have the UI designer and front end developer revise the website. Further tests will be needed, but the process will be limited by the website launch deadline and development budget.

The UX designer will often supplement the wireframe design with other deliverables to help guide the website design. One of these deliverables is known as "personas." Personas are a series of descriptions of potential product and website users—their ages, genders, likes, dislikes, and interests. The UX designer creates these descriptions based on interviews and surveys conducted during the research phase and user testing. The web development team uses personas to better target the potential audience for the website. Another popular tool is the storyboard. A storyboard is a series of pictures, often drawn like a comic strip, depicting the user's journey through the website and with the company's product. A storyboard "may be an extremely rough sketch—purely for crystallising your own ideas—or a more polished comic for engaging your audience more effectively," explains Magain. "Depending on the audience, a storyboard may be a more appropriate tool for capturing how, when, where and why someone might use your product."

How Do You Become a User Experience Designer?

Education

Most companies expect a UX designer to have at least a bachelor's degree. A survey of 1,355 UX designers conducted by the User Experience Professionals Association (UXPA) found that 60 percent of UX designers have advanced degrees, with 53 percent holding master's degrees and 7 percent holding PhDs. Of the remaining 40 percent, 33 percent held bachelor's degrees. Among the 7 percent who did not have a college degree, about half held a technical or an associate's degree and about half held a high school diploma.

A survey by Nielsen Norman Group (NNG) found that 90 percent of UX designers hold at least a bachelor's degree, although the survey revealed a wide range of study areas among UX designers, including design, psychology, communications, English, and computer science. "All of these fields make some sense as a partial educational

User experience designers often work with the marketing team to develop and analyze customer surveys and interviews. The goal is to enhance interaction between the customer and the company through its website and products.

background for UX professionals," wrote Jakob Nielsen and Susan Farrell of NNG in an article on the NNG website, "but together those five disciplines accounted for only 15 percent of bachelor's degrees. The majority of UX professionals hold degrees from an immense range of other disciplines, from history to chemistry, most of which don't have a direct bearing on UX work."

Certification

UX designers are not required to be licensed or certified, but many UX designers obtain certification to demonstrate they understand the principles of UX design and have experience doing it. This is particularly helpful because UX design is a relatively new field, and not everyone agrees on what it entails.

Certification in UX design is available from many online training companies, including NNG, which offers UX and UX Master

Certification Programs, and General Assembly, a programming and coding boot camp that offers User Experience Design Immersive certification. Some colleges and universities offer certification as well. For example, California State University at Fullerton offers a Certificate in User Experience and Customer-Centered Design; the University of California at San Diego Extension offers a User Experience (UX) Design Certificate; and University of Baltimore offers a Certificate in User Experience (UX) Design.

Internships

A search of Indeed.com in July 2016 returned 196 listings for UX designer interns, mostly for those enrolled in college. Many of these positions were with software development companies that need help with product development. However, many of the skills and techniques used in product development are the same as for website development. For example, ServiceMax, which markets a cloud-based sales management platform, advertised on the website Indeed.com for a UX design intern who would "help the team with production tasks, including creation of high-fidelity mockups based on wireframes and style guides. Whether you're building input forms, splash screens, or launch icons, your creativity will be an important input into the look and feel of the finished product."

Skills and Personality

UX designers work in the field of human-machine interaction, but the majority of what they do has more to do with humans than with machines. "UX Design is more about working with people than working on your own in front of a screen," writes Magain. Whether acquired through formal education, self-education, or work experience, UX designers need to understand the way people think—known as cognitive psychology—and how their thinking affects their interaction with computers. UX designers need excellent oral and written language skills so they can conduct interviews and surveys and summarize their findings in reports, personas, and scenarios. They also need to be able to communicate and coordinate with UI designers, front end developers, clients, or stakeholders. "We do a little bit of market research, a little bit of psychology. We're synthesizers, pulling bits and pieces of different methodologies together," UX designer Whitney Quesenbery told *Computerworld*.

On the technical side, the UX designer needs to learn to use UX design tools for wireframing and prototyping. Among the most popular are UXPin, which allows the designer to create responsive clickable prototypes on a browser; Pixate, which allows the designer to test complex mobile interactions, animations, and transitions; Axure, a complete wireframing and protoyping software; and Mockups.me, which allows designers to quickly create interactive wireframes on a tablet.

Employers

Although the principles of UX design can be applied to any industry, the vast majority of UX design positions are in the digital field. Apple and Facebook are two of the best-known companies that employ large numbers of UX designers.

Working Conditions

UX designers work indoors in a casual environment. On days when conducting face-to-face interviews, product testing, or client meetings, the UX designer may be required to dress in business casual or business attire. Most positions are full time, although schedules can vary depending on workloads and deadlines. According to the UXPA, almost all UX designers work for companies; only 1 percent reported being self-employed.

Earnings

A salary survey conducted by the UXPA revealed the median salary of UX designers to be $92,500, with designers at the lower end earning about $61,000 and designers at the high end earning $137,000. Salaries for UX designers vary greatly by geographic location. According to Onward Search, UX designers in San Jose, in the heart of Silicon Valley, can earn up to $137,000 a year; while the top of the UX designer salary range is $82,000 in Pittsburgh, $87,000 in Phoenix, and $91,000 in Minneapolis. Salary also varies by the highest educational degree attained. According to the UXPA, UX designers with a PhD earned a median of $120,000 a year; those with a master's degree earned a median of $95,000 a year, while those with a high school diploma or bachelor's degree earned up to $92,000 a year.

Opportunities for Advancement

An experienced UX designer has many opportunities for advancement. A UX designer can become a user experience director, a user-centered design manager, a usability director, or a user experience researcher.

What Is the Future Outlook for User Experience Designers?

User experience design is one of the hottest areas of product and web development. According to Brazen, a recruitment agency in Washington, DC, UX design is the highest out of seven in-demand careers for design and planning, with job growth up to 30 percent. "Because design and planning play such an essential role in our lives, it's no surprise employers are looking to hire in these innovative industries," digital marketer Annie Favreau writes on the Brazen blog. CNN Money pegs UX designer job growth at 18 percent over the next ten years.

Find Out More

Human Factors and Ergonomics Society
PO Box 1369
Santa Monica, CA 90406
website: www.hfes.org

The Human Factors and Ergonomics Society advocates systematic use of knowledge concerning human characteristics to achieve compatibility in the design of interactive systems of people, machines, and environments to ensure their effectiveness, safety, and ease of performance. It offers publications, a career center, events, and a library of recorded webinars.

Interaction Design Association (IxDA)
website: www.ixda.org

The IxDA, a global network of more than eighty thousand members and more than 173 local groups, is a member-supported organization dedicated to the discipline of interaction design. The association holds an interaction conference and an education summit and sponsors awards for professionals and a student design challenge. Its website features a jobs listing and a discussion group.

Special Interest Group on Computer-Human Interaction (SIGCHI)
119 E. Union St., Suite A
Pasadena, CA 91103
website: www.sigchi.org

The SIGCHI is an international society for professionals, academics, and students who are interested in human-technology and human-computer interaction. A subgroup of the Association for Computing Machinery, the organization offers publications, hosts message boards, and holds conferences in the multidisciplinary field of human-computer interaction.

User Experience Professionals Association (UXPA)
website: http://uxpa.org

The UXPA supports people who research, design, and evaluate the user experience of products and services. UXPA holds yearly international conferences and publishes new findings through journals. The association facilitates professional development and education within the UX field. Its website features a job board, a discussion board, and a directory of consultants.

Web Developer

What Does a Web Developer Do?

The World Wide Web consists of 13 billion interconnected web pages. These pages may display words, pictures, graphics, or videos, and often link to other pages or to software programs. Every page is written in a programming language, or code, that the Internet user's browser can read and display. The people who write this code are known as web developers. The web pages that are visible to an Internet user are created by a person known as a front end, or client-side, web developer. The part of the page that connects to other computers behind the scenes is built by a person known as a back end, or server-side, web developer. Some people have both front end and back end development skills. They are known as full stack developers, because they can work with the full "stack" of technology.

The job of the front end developer is to translate the vision of the client, web designer, or user experience designer into programming language that Internet browsers can read and back end developers can use as a launching pad for additional applications. Front end developers use three programming languages to control how web pages

At a Glance:
Web Developer

Minimum Educational Requirements
Associate's degree or equivalent

Personal Qualities
Creative problem solving; detail oriented; passionate about the web

Certification and Licensing
Voluntary

Working Conditions
Indoors

Salary Range
About $34,000 to $117,000

Number of Jobs
As of 2014 about 148,500

Future Job Outlook
Growth rate of 27 percent through 2024

look and function: Hypertext Markup Language (HTML), which browsers read and display; Cascading Style Sheets (CSS) that control the presentation of multiple HTML pages without having to write code for the same design elements on each one; and JavaScript, which enables the developer to create dynamic, interactive elements such as drop-down menus and sliders. "It doesn't take a long time to learn HTML and CSS, but it takes a lifetime to master them," Michael Thomas, chief technology officer of mtwebink, a UK web development company, says in a YouTube video.

The back end developer creates software programs that connect the interactive portions of the client-side page to applications and data residing on one or more computers that are part of the host organization's network. For example, a bank's web page might connect an online customer to his or her account information, which is stored in a database on a networked computer. The customer is able to access the database to perform a transaction, such as paying a bill or transferring funds to another account. The software applications that enable these transactions to occur and that display the updated information are created by a back end developer. "We call back-end code the brain of any app out there," writes Doug Manning, president of Manning Digital, in his blog.

> The developer builds an application (using server-side code like PHP, Ruby, Python, .Net etc.) which connects with a database (using MySQL, SQL, Access etc.) to look up, save or change data and return it back to the user in the form of front-end code. This complicated structure helps us look for things, shop, interact socially and more in the modern world of the Internet.

Front end and back end web developers work together closely, often using the same software frameworks—time-saving software tools that sometimes include generic code that can be used for simple functions. They also both may use content management systems—such as WordPress, Perch, ExpressionEngine, and Drupal—that create a platform on which to develop website applications. As a result, many front end developers know something about back end development, and vice versa.

Web developers write the code that makes it possible for Internet users to browse, read, and use the billions of interconnected pages that make up the World Wide Web. Some developers specialize in one aspect of web page creation while others have expertise in multiple areas.

Some companies, such as Facebook, find it desirable for their web developers to be full stack developers, possessing both the front end and back end programming skills. "Full stack developers offer the full package," writes Michael Wales, director of learning at Udacity, on the company's blog. "Full stack developers should be knowledgeable in every level of how the web works: setting up and configuring Linux servers, writing server-side APIs [application program interfaces], diving into the client-side JavaScript powering an application, and turning a 'design eye' to the CSS." Being a full stack developer can be an advantage when seeking a job, especially in a slow economy, when companies are looking for ways to limit the number of people they employ.

How Do You Become a Web Developer?

Education

There is no set educational path to becoming a web developer. A person who can write good, lean code for either the front end or the back end of a website is employable. "For a front-end developer, you don't need a degree," Andy Orin, a front end developer for Jobvite, a software recruiting firm, writes on the Lifehacker website. "Your work kind of shows how much you know. A lot of people these days are self-taught." A strong portfolio is a must, whether a person has a degree or not. The sample websites the developer has built will reveal a great deal about his or her knowledge and skills.

Many companies require web developers to have at least an associate's degree in software development, computer science, or a related field. Larger companies and government offices may require candidates to have a bachelor's degree, although it does not have to be in a technical field. David Kalt, the founder of Reverb, an online marketplace for musical instruments and gear, told the *Wall Street Journal*: "Looking back at the tech teams that I've built at my companies, it's evident that individuals with liberal arts degrees are by far the sharpest, best-performing software developers and technology leaders. Often these modern techies have degrees in philosophy, history, and music—even political science, which was my degree." The key, he says, is that a liberal arts education develops critical thinking. "Critical thinkers can accomplish anything. Critical thinkers can master French, Ruby on Rails, Python or whatever future language comes their way. A critical thinker is a self-learning machine that is not constrained by memorizing commands or syntax."

Certification and Licensing

Many organizations—technical schools, community colleges, university extension programs, professional organizations, and software

companies—offer certification for proficiency in website development, software tools, and programming languages. For example,
Microsoft Corporation was the first company to offer an entry-level
credential for HTML5, the latest version of the markup language
used for front end web development. Certifications can help a web
developer's résumé or online profile stand out.

Volunteer Work and Internships

Since a portfolio of work is essential for a web developer to find a
job, many beginning web developers volunteer to build websites for
small businesses or organizations just so they can show their work
to future employers. Companies looking to enhance their websites or
assist their marketing teams sometimes offer unpaid internships to
beginning web developers. Internships are an excellent way to make
contacts in the industry that could lead to a paying position.

Skills and Personality

While web development is a technical field, web developers must have
excellent interpersonal skills as well. Front end developers work with
back end developers, and vice versa; and both work with web designers, interactive content producers, database administrators, systems
architects, and many others. Communication is vital to the success of
any project. In addition, web developers often meet with clients and
stakeholders to understand what the website is intended to achieve.
Web developers need to be able to describe what is technically possible to nontechnical people so everyone can agree on how a website
should look and function.

Both front end and back end developers must be fascinated by
websites—how they look and function—and have a deep desire to
build them. They also must be detail oriented, since writing code
is very exacting, and even a single coding error can cause a page to
malfunction or not load at all. They also must enjoy learning new
things and acquiring new skills. "Since the world of web development
changes as rapidly as the Internet does, these experts are constantly
learning and training," writes Shannon Lee, a reporter for MSN
Money, on the company's website.

On the Job

Employers

Almost every company, nonprofit organization, and school has a website—or wants one. As a result, web developers are in high demand. According to the Bureau of Labor Statistics (BLS), the industries employing the largest number of web developers are computer systems design and related services; educational services; religious, civic, professional, and similar organizations; and non-Internet publishing.

The BLS also reports that 14 percent of web developers are self-employed—a higher percentage than many other professions. A self-employed web developer normally is hired to complete a project—such as building and testing the front end of a website—for a certain amount of money, regardless of how many hours the job takes. This position offers the web developer the greatest flexibility for work hours, but it also can be stressful, because the developer must constantly find new clients in order to work steadily.

Some web developers are contract employees—a position that lies between working full-time for a company and being self-employed. Contract workers are employed by consulting firms, often in the IT field or marketing field. The consulting firm finds the clients, secures the job, and then divides the work among various specialists. The contract web developer usually works on site at the consulting firm and is paid an hourly rate, as in a permanent job, but without medical and other benefits. Being a contract web developer offers more variety than a permanent position does and allows the web developer to concentrate on coding—rather than on finding and maintaining a stream of clients, as a self-employed web developer must.

Working Conditions

Web developers work indoors, often in a casual office environment. Members of a web development team usually work in close proximity so they can discuss the project and view each other's computer screens. Web developers often are required to work overtime to meet internal and client deadlines. They also must be on call at all hours in case something goes wrong with the website and must be fixed.

Earnings

According to the BLS, the median annual wage for web developers in 2015 was $64,970. The top 10 percent earned more than $116,000 a year, and the bottom 10 percent earned less than $34,770. Web developers earn 80 percent more than the median salary of all other occupations, but about 20 percent less than the median salary for all other computer occupations.

Opportunities for Advancement

Most companies offer three levels of web development positions: junior web developer, web developer, and senior web developer. After that senior web developers can move into management as a project leader or the manager of a development department. Some senior web developers go into business on their own, founding consulting firms or working as freelance consultants.

What Is the Future Outlook for Web Developers?

The BLS forecasts that the number of web development positions will increase by 27 percent by 2023, much faster than the average for all occupations. The forecast is based in part on the fact retail firms are expected to expand their online offerings in the coming years. Because of the phenomenal growth in smartphone usage, web developers are needed to launch phone-friendly websites or redesign existing web pages into smartphone formats.

Find Out More

International Webmasters Association (IWA)
119 E. Union St., Suite A
Pasadena, CA 91103
website: http://iwanet.org

Founded in 1996 the IWA is one of the leading organizations for web professionals. It provides education programs such as its Certified Web

Professional program. Its website also contains a list of job profiles and professional standards.

Webgrrls International
119 W. Seventy-Second St., #314
New York, NY 10023
website: www.webgrrls.com

Founded in 1995 to empower women through technology, Webgrrls International is an online and offline networking organization of professional women who work with the web. The site includes a networking area, group discussion forum, events calendar, jobs bank, industry blog, and various educational materials.

WebProfessionals.org
website: www.webprofessionals.org

WebProfessionals.org is a nonprofit professional association dedicated to the support of individuals and organizations who create, manage, or market websites. The organization provides education, training, and certification for those who aspire to become web professionals, those who already are web professionals, and those who teach web professionals.

Search Engine Optimization Manager

What Does a Search Engine Optimization Manager Do?

At a Glance:

Search Engine Optimization Manager

Minimum Educational Requirements
Bachelor's degree; graduate degree a plus

Personal Qualities
Highly analytical; passionate about SEO; excellent communication skills

Certification and Licensing
Certification preferred

Working Conditions
Indoors, onsite or remote

Salary Range
About $47,000 to $153,000

Number of Jobs
As of 2014 about 6,000

Future Job Outlook
Growth rate of 15 percent through 2024

Many people visit websites by following direct links in news stories, blogs, and social media such as Facebook and Twitter, but the vast majority of Internet users find pages via search engines such as Google, Bing, or Yahoo. The Internet users type text—known as keywords—into a field in the search engine; commonplace keywords often return thousands if not millions of results. Most search engines will show ten results per page. Since 80 percent of Internet users look only at the first page of results, competition to show up on the first page of results is fierce. To companies that sell most or all of their products online, ranking in the top search results is a matter of corporate life or death. These companies often employ search engine optimization (SEO) experts to lead a multipronged effort to improve a website's ranking for keywords related to their business.

An SEO manager's responsibilities are broken into two main categories: on-page and off-page optimization. On-page SEO involves editing the Hypertext Markup Language (HTML) code that is used to create web pages so the search engines can "understand" what the page is about and, in turn, rank it accordingly. The SEO manager must keep up-to-date on how the website's HTML interacts with software programs known as search engine robots, or bots. The bots analyze the website, gathering the data that determines search engine ranking. For example, bots cannot "see" pictures; they only read text. As a result, each picture on a web page should have a written description of what it shows. This description should include a keyword the SEO manager wants the website to rank for when the company is searched by a user. The SEO manager makes sure the keywords are strategically placed on each page—for example, in the first headline and initial body text. However, placing too many keywords on a page or placing them in the wrong places on a page can lead to the website being penalized in the search engine rankings. If the SEO manager uses misleading tactics to try to increase the page's ranking, a search engine like Google might remove the website from the search engine's results altogether.

An SEO manager also spends a great deal of time on off-page SEO work. This includes building inbound links to pages of the website from outside sources. For example, it is very beneficial for a website dedicated to one topic to obtain links from other websites dedicated to the same topic. Inbound links are considered "votes" by the search engines. The more votes a page receives, the better it can rank in the search engine results. Inbound links can be obtained from a variety of sources, such as news articles, business partner websites, social shares on Twitter, and many more. Just like on-page optimization, overdoing this can also result in penalties from the search engines. The SEO manager must make sure all inbound links make sense and do not represent efforts to "game the system." Some of the best inbound links come from impartial sources, such as traditional news outlets, so the SEO manager often spends time building relationships with members of the media so they write about and link to the website.

An SEO manager uses online tools and software to measure the success of SEO campaigns, prepare reports, perform audits of website activity, and document results. For example, an SEO manager will use software tools to find out where the traffic to the website came from, which search engines people used, or which links people followed to get to the website. The SEO manager will also study the keywords people are using to find the company's or client's website and others like it. The results of this research will guide the SEO manager toward developing a strategy to improve search engine ranking and web traffic. "One of the things I enjoy most about SEO is that it's never boring," writes Julie Joyce, owner of Link Fish Media, a company that specializes in SEO, on the Link-Assistant.com blog. "There's always something to test and there's always something more to learn."

SEO managers must keep up-to-date with the constantly changing search engine algorithms—the set of step-by-step operations performed by the computer—that produce the search results. "With an average of two daily algorithm tweaks Google keeps us on our toes at all times," Dan Petrovic, owner of DEJAN SEO in Australia, writes on the Link-Assistant.com blog. "Search engines (particularly Google) have grown very complex with a myriad of new variables at play. This means that if you're not agile, creative, analytical and a little bit scientific by nature, you'll hardly succeed in a big way."

The search engine companies keep their algorithms secret, so the SEO manager is like a detective who conducts tests and follows clues to find out how rankings are currently being determined. The SEO manager then either makes changes on the website or adjusts the off-page strategy to keep up with the changing search environment.

How Do You Become a Search Engine Optimization Manager?

Education

Different employers have different educational requirements for SEO managers. Corporations often require a bachelor's degree, while smaller firms might require an associate's degree. A communications, business, or marketing background is often preferred but not required. Whatever their background, SEO managers need to demonstrate they have acquired strong analytical and communication skills.

Certification and Licensing

Although SEO managers do not need to know how to create websites, they need to be able to read and edit HTML code so they can optimize the page for search engine ranking. Many universities, technical schools, professional organizations, online schools, and software companies offer certification in HTML. This certification can be particularly useful if the would-be SEO manager comes from a nontechnical background. Several organizations offer certification in SEO best practices, strategy, and advanced techniques. For example, SEOcertification.org offers certification as an SEO Certified Professional.

Volunteer Work and Internships

Everyone with a website wants it to rank higher in search engine results, so offering to make that happen at no charge is almost always welcomed. Taking screen shots of a website's search rankings before and after the volunteer project to document improvements can make a compelling case that the SEO manager knows what he or she is doing. Many small businesses make basic SEO mistakes, and fixing these can immediately improve rankings.

Several companies offer internships for off-page SEO work, such as creating online content with hyperlinks back to the company website. This link-building experience is extremely helpful to would-be SEO managers because they become familiar with some of the best online locations for posting SEO copy.

Skills and Personality

SEO managers must be highly analytical and enjoy spending their time creating, running, and analyzing reports. Strong written and verbal communication skills and be familiar with various software tools such as Google Analytics or Google AdWords—a keyword tool that aids with the analysis of search trends. They also must enjoy acquiring new knowledge and skills to keep pace with the ever-changing world of search engine optimization. "SEO is dynamic; as Google and other search engines continue to refine their algorithms, they change the way SEO is planned and carried out," Nancy E. Wigal, owner of Search Engine Academy Washington DC, an SEO training and consulting firm, explains on the Link-Assistant.com blog. "Anyone who wants to do SEO will never be bored."

On the Job

Employers

Only large corporations that depend on the Internet for much of their business have marketing needs and budgets large enough to employ SEO managers full time. Known as "in-house SEOs," these positions are growing in number every year as companies realize the importance of search engine optimization. Many SEO managers also work for web development companies, and their services are part of the package deal that clients receive when their websites are built and maintained. These SEO managers make sure that each page is bot friendly and the highlighted keywords serve the overall marketing strategy. The client also might pay for ongoing off-page link building, search testing, and analysis.

Many advertising agencies and new media companies employ SEO managers as part of the services they offer. Businesses engage these marketing companies not only to increase awareness of their brands and products but also to boost traffic to their websites and, eventually, to increase sales. The fastest way to increase website visits is to improve a website's search engine ranking for the keywords that likely buyers associate with the company and its products and services. "[SEO] is a big, broad, scary profession where, when you make a mistake, everyone knows about it and they know it's you. But when you have great successes, it's dollars and cents for your clients and your company," Troy Boileau, an SEO manager with Powered by Search, a Canadian Internet marketing firm, writes on the Link-Assistant.com blog.

Working Conditions

SEO managers work indoors, at a desk with a computer. SEO managers in large corporations typically work in a highly structured environment, with professional dress codes and regular hours. Those who work for web development companies and marketing firms often work in a more casual environment with more flexible hours. However, SEO managers often meet with clients, so they might be required to dress professionally on these occasions.

Earnings

According to Indeed.com, the average SEO manager earns about $90,000 a year. Some similar positions pay more, and others pay less. For example, a web commerce manager earns about $157,000 a year, while an SEO technical manager, who specializes in on-page optimization, earns about $47,000. Salaries for in-house SEO positions within large companies like Amazon, Intuit, eBay, and others, range from $80,000 to $165,000.

Opportunities for Advancement

An SEO manager has a lot of room for advancement, with opportunities to work with or manage small to large teams, or even start an SEO marketing company. Some companies offer a senior SEO manager position. After that, senior SEO managers might move into marketing management, either with specific products or with e-commerce in general. Starting an SEO company can be an excellent move, because nearly all companies that have websites have a strong desire to improve their search rankings.

What Is the Future Outlook for Search Engine Optimization Managers?

Some people believe the day will come when the algorithms used by search engines for ranking websites are so efficient that they will not be influenced by the strategies employed by SEO managers, spelling the end of the profession. Most SEO professionals disagree. "As long as websites, search and the Internet exists, so will SEO," Gerald Weber, founder of Search Engine Marketing Group in Houston, Texas, told the Link-Assistant.com blog. "Don't ever listen to SEO naysayers who cry 'SEO is dead . . . the sky is falling. . . .' SEO has definitely changed and will continue to do so, but it will never go away or not be in demand."

Moz
1100 Second Ave., Suite 500
Seattle, WA 98101
website: https://moz.com

An SEO software vendor, Moz provides valuable free information on its website, including white papers ranging from beginner's guides to advanced SEO topics. The website includes a discussion forum; visitors also can use a free online tool that shows how many inbound links a website has, how many pages it has, and keywords most commonly used to link to the domain.

National Center for Women & Information Technology
1125 Eighteenth St.
Boulder, CO 80309
website: www.ncwit.org

The National Center for Women & Information Technology is a nonprofit organization that works with public and private organizations to increase girls' and women's participation in technology and computing. The center helps organizations with computing staffing needs to recruit, retain, and advance women by providing support, evidence, and action.

Search Engine Land
website: http://searchengineland.com

Search Engine Land is a daily publication that covers all aspects of the search marketing industry. Coverage includes SEO and pay per click news, search engine updates, and industry trends. The website provides tips, tactics, and strategies for running successful search marketing campaigns. The organization also sponsors conferences and webcasts.

SEMPO
401 Edgewater Pl., Suite 600
Wakefield, MA 01880
website: www.sempo.org

SEMPO is a global nonprofit organization serving the search engine marketing industry. Its goal is to provide education for its members, promote the industry, generate research, and create a better understanding of search and its role in marketing. It offers an extensive library of resources, research and articles, and activities such as webinars and speaking events.

Database Administrator

What Does a Database Administrator Do?

Nearly every company doing business on the Internet stores information about its products, pricing, and customers in a database—a large collection of data accessible by a computer. For example, Amazon maintains a database of all of the books, videos, and other items it sells. This database is searchable by visitors to the website. Other companies, such as eBay, do not have products, but earn money by maintaining a database of items other people have to sell and then charging a small commission when sales are made. Many online companies and social media outlets maintain databases that are constantly being accessed by users. A database administrator (DBA) is responsible for the design, implementation, maintenance, and modification of databases.

DBAs often are involved in the planning and development of online databases. DBAs meet with members of the marketing, finance, production, or other

---

At a Glance:

Database Administrator

Minimum Educational Requirements
Bachelor's degree

Personal Qualities
Strong analytical skills; detail oriented

Certification and Licensing
Often required for specific database management systems

Working Conditions
Indoors

Salary Range
About $45,500 to $127,000

Number of Jobs
As of 2014 about 120,000

Future Job Outlook
Growth rate of 11 percent through 2024

areas of the company to establish the company's needs. The DBA then maps out the conceptual design for a planned database, taking into consideration both back end organization of the data and front end accessibility for end users. Once the plan is approved, the DBA translates the design into a working model, and may further refine the physical design to meet system storage requirements. The DBA makes sure the organization's data is clearly defined and consistently formatted across the database so users can find and access all records. The DBA then tests and monitors the system until it appears ready to use. Throughout the process, the DBA takes notes to create documentation that includes the standards and procedures used to create the database.

After the database programming is complete, the DBA constantly monitors the database to make sure it is working efficiently. For example, the DBA makes certain that multiple users can access the database at the same time without conflicts or disruptions. In the event that efficiency has been degraded, the DBA must troubleshoot and fix the problem. "The primary task of database administrators is to maintain the stability of the database," writes Matthew Morris, an author of more than twenty study guides for Oracle certification exams, for *Certification Magazine*, an online publication. "In general, if the database is doing the exact same thing on Friday that it was on Monday, the administrator has done his or her job (obviously this assumes the database was running correctly on Monday). Much of what administrators do is a cyclical routine of ensuring that everything is happening as expected."

The DBA also is responsible for the security of the database, either personally or in partnership with security analysts. For example, some of the greatest threats to the security of a database come not from people outside the company—such as hackers—but by people within the company who unintentionally degrade database performance by running poorly designed queries and operations. The DBA not only must monitor the system to detect such errors, but also train colleagues in how to input and extract data. In the event that the database is corrupted, the DBA is responsible for having a backup copy of the database that can be retrieved for disaster recovery. The DBA develops, manages, and tests backup and disaster recovery plans.

"Being a DBA is like a being a ninja; never seen, never heard, but are always there to . . . save the day," Colin Stasiuk, an independent DBA consultant in Canada, told the author in an interview. "I love what I do," Stasiuk adds on his website. "It has not only provided a great life for myself and my family, but it has given me the ability and skillset to help protect the most important asset of a company: its data."

How Do You Become a Database Administrator?

Education

Most companies require database administrators to have a bachelor's degree in management information systems or a computer-related field. Companies with large databases often prefer candidates who have a master's degree in computer science, information technology, or database management.

Many DBAs do not start out in the profession, but rather are promoted into it, having gained the necessary knowledge as database developers—software developers who specialize in creating database applications—or as data analysts, who work with databases to generate reports. DBAs also might gain their database knowledge from positions in computer operations or IT support. "Colleges turn out people who can build databases from a textbook, but all the analysis and design that goes into building a database [at the business level] is hard to learn in college. These are mostly things learned on the job," Loretta Mahon Smith, former vice president of communications for Data Management Association (DAMA) International, a nonprofit association for technical and business professionals, told *U.S. News & World Report*.

Certification and Licensing

Different companies use different relational database management systems (RDBMS) such as MySQL, Oracle, and DB2; and a DBA is expected to be certified in the use of the one his or her employer uses. The software companies that provide the database management systems usually offer certification in the use of their products. For example, software vendor Oracle offers certification as an Oracle Database Administrator Certified Professional, and Microsoft offers certification as a Certified Database Administrator for SQL servers. Certification demonstrates that the DBA understands the best practices required to maximize the use of the software.

Volunteer Work and Internships

A company's database is one of the most valuable things it owns, and keeping it safe is one of a company's highest priorities. As a result, companies rarely if ever place such an important asset in the hands of a volunteer or intern. Most volunteers are experienced professionals or retirees who offer their expertise to nonprofit or religious organizations that have limited budgets but great need for a well-designed and efficient database.

Skills and Personality

DBAs need to have strong analytical skills so they can evaluate a database system's performance and know when to take action to keep it operating at maximum efficiency. Because problems with the database often must be fixed while the system is running, DBAs must be able to work quickly and under pressure. They must have excellent problem-solving skills and enjoy troubleshooting and correcting problems. DBAs must be able to think logically so they can organize data in a way that can be retrieved with the least use of system resources.

DBAs typically are part of an IT team, and must be able to communicate effectively with software developers, web developers, managers, and others. However, they also must be comfortable working alone for long periods of time as they fine-tune, upgrade, and test modifications to the databases. DBAs often perform large-scale tasks such as updating and amending existing databases, merging databases, or creating new ones. These projects must be completed within specific time frames, so DBAs need to be able to manage their time so they can meet deadlines.

DBAs must have a deep understanding of Structured Query Language (SQL), the main language used to extract data from a database. They also need to understand various database management systems such as RDBMS, object-oriented database management systems (OODBMS), and Extensible Markup Language (XML) database management systems. Those DBAs who work for Internet companies must understand how the database interacts with various web applications.

On the Job

Employers

Nearly all organizations—from the largest corporations to small- and medium-sized enterprises—collect and retain data about their customers, members, suppliers, products, and services. In addition, businesses are trying to make greater use of their databases to retain their customers and attract new ones, using a process known as customer relationship management. DBAs can find an opportunity within any organization that uses computerized databases, including organizations in both the public and private sectors. According to the Bureau of Labor Statistics (BLS), 15 percent of DBAs work for computer system design companies and related computing services. About 11 percent of DBAs work in educational services at the state, local, and private levels. About 7 percent work in the insurance industry.

Many DBAs work as freelance consultants or contractors. For example, a small-to-medium-sized company might hire a freelance DBA to design and develop a relatively small database, while an IT consulting firm might hire a DBA to work on a large-scale project along with other consultants and specialists. Working as a consultant requires the DBA to understand and have experience with various database management systems. DBA consultants can command a higher salary than full-time employees, and they can take off time between contracts. However, independent contractors must arrange for their own benefits, such as health insurance and retirement.

Working Conditions

DBAs work indoors at their desks, working on a computer. According to the BLS, about one in five DBAs worked more than forty hours per week in 2014. DBAs often are required to work overnight or weekends as maintenance sometimes needs to be performed during periods of low usage. DBAs are usually on call in case a critical problem occurs. Since many DBAs work in corporate settings, they often are expected to follow a business casual dress code.

Earnings

According to the BLS, the median annual wage for DBAs in 2015 was $81,710. The top 10 percent earned more than $127,000 a year, and the bottom 10 percent earned less than $45,460. DBAs earn more than twice the median salary as that of all other occupations, and almost exactly the median of all other computer occupations. Indeed.com lists the average salary of a DBA at $58,000 as of June 2016, with a senior DBA making $153,000 a year at the high end and an entry-level DBA making $26,000 at the low end. CNN Money pegged the median pay for a DBA at $120,000 in 2015, with the top pay at $152,000.

Opportunities for Advancement

DBAs can use their database knowledge, planning, and time-management skills to become IT managers, who are in charge of planning, coordinating, and directing any computer-related activities for a company. Some DBAs become database specialists in the area of interactive web-based databases. Such specialists often move into self-employment or consultancy work, sometimes subcontracting with data hosting, data processing, or web development companies.

What Is the Future Outlook for Database Administrators?

The growing use of the Internet to conduct business leads analysts to believe that the number of online databases and the demand for DBAs will continue to grow at a fast rate. The BLS estimates the job market for DBAs to grow by 11 percent through 2024, which the bureau describes as faster than average. CNN Money is even more optimistic, forecasting a 15 percent growth in DBA positions through 2025.

Find Out More

Association for Computing Machinery (ACM)
2 Penn Plaza, Suite 701
New York, NY 10121
website: www.acm.org

With more than one hundred thousand members worldwide, the ACM is the world's largest educational and scientific computing society. Its goal is to deliver resources that advance computing as both a science and a profession. The ACM maintains the computing field's premier digital library and provides its members with publications, conferences, and career resources.

Data Administration Newsletter (TDAN.com)
PO Box 112571
Pittsburgh, PA 15241
website: http://tdan.com

TDAN.com is an online publication for people who have the responsibility for managing data as a valued organizational asset. It contains articles and resources for data management professionals and those considering a career in the industry. It also includes an archive of companies and products, books and book reviews, and event listings.

Data Management Association (DAMA) International
website: www.dama.org

DAMA International is a not-for-profit global association of technical and business professionals. Its educational programs are dedicated to advancing the concepts and practices of data management through research, education, publications, promotion of standards, and other activities. DAMA International offers a certification program for DBAs.

International DB2 Users Group (IDUG)
330 N. Wabash, Suite 2000
Chicago, IL 60611
website: www.idug.org

An independent not-for-profit organization, IDUG provides education and services to promote use of DB2, IBM's database server product. The organization holds industry conferences and technical seminars. Its website includes user forums, industry news and blogs, and a technical library. Some areas of the site are open only to members, but membership is free.

SearchDataManagement
website: http://searchdatamanagement.techtarget.com

SearchDataManagement is a website that provides news, learning guides, expert advice, and webcasts to data management professionals. The site offers independent and vendor-produced content about various database management products. It also has a large archive of articles and podcasts of interest to IT professionals and those seeking a career in data management.

Cybersecurity Analyst

What Does a Cybersecurity Analyst Do?

Companies and government offices that do business on the Internet run the risk of having their databases accessed, copied, or changed by unauthorized users known as hackers. In addition hackers who gain access to a computer network can bring it to a halt, forcing an online business to go dark until the problem is solved. Many organizations hire highly trained professionals known as cybersecurity analysts to thwart these high-tech intruders and protect their databases and computer operations from such attacks. A cybersecurity analyst plans and implements security measures to prevent hackers from gaining access to the system. They also monitor the organization's system so they can react quickly when a security breach occurs and prevent damage.

Cyberattacks have been on the rise around the globe, with hackers targeting public and private computer systems connected to the Internet to steal

At a Glance:
Cybersecurity Analyst

Minimum Educational Requirements
Bachelor's degree or equivalent

Personal Qualities
Ingenuity; creativity; problem solving

Certification and Licensing
Greatly preferred

Working Conditions
Indoors

Salary Range
About $51,000 to $144,000

Number of Jobs
As of 2014 about 82,900

Future Job Outlook
Growth rate of 18 percent through 2024

information or bring computer networks to a halt. For example, in February 2016 the US Internal Revenue Service (IRS) reported that hackers had copied the data from more than seven hundred thousand taxpayer accounts and had used the data to file fifteen thousand fraudulent tax returns and receive $55 million in federal tax refunds. Banks such as JPMorgan Chase; retail chains including Target, Home Depot, and T.J. Maxx/Marshalls; social media companies such as LinkedIn and Tumblr; and health care insurers such as Anthem have all been hacked and had valuable records stolen. As a result of these and other attacks, cybersecurity has become a major concern for every online enterprise.

Cybersecurity analysts plan and implement security measures to protect computer systems, networks, and data. They often purchase, install, and test software tools designed to prevent intruders from gaining access to the system. These tools include firewalls (software programs that inspect incoming data before allowing it to pass into the organization's network); personal identification systems that allow only credentialed users to access the system; network intrusion detection systems that monitor the traffic to and from all of the connected devices in a network; and data encryption software that prevents hackers from reading the data even if they access it.

On a typical day cybersecurity analysts use various software tools to monitor their organizations' networks, watching for unusual changes in activity that can signal an intruder is present. They also receive reports from various sources—such as database administrators—that might alert them to a possible breach in security.

If a security violation occurs, the cybersecurity analyst investigates. If security has been breached, the cybersecurity analyst takes steps to protect sensitive information. The cybersecurity analyst might use a Host intrusion detection system (HIDS) to determine if any files have been changed or deleted. Since the HIDS keeps a log of all data flowing in and out of a device, the cybersecurity analyst can use the log to trace the source of the intrusion. The cybersecurity analyst must then prepare a report that documents the security breach and the extent of the damage it caused. If data has been lost or corrupted or the network has been disrupted, the cybersecurity analyst will work with the vendor or colleagues within the organization responsible for backup and disaster recovery to restore the lost data.

If everything appears to be running normally, the cybersecurity analyst might conduct penetration testing, probing the system the way a hacker might to identify vulnerabilities before they can be exploited. Cybersecurity analysts must keep up-to-date on the latest security trends and intelligence, including hackers' methodologies, and then simulate such attacks on their own systems to see if they work. "Read voraciously on the topic (news as well as tech stuff)," advises David Gewirtz, a computer scientist, US policy advisor, and author, on the ZDNet website. "The more you know, the more you'll know who to try reaching out to. That's good advice for pretty much anything, but it works here, too. Don't just read technical information, but dive deeply into each individual case and learn about the business ramifications and how the actual breaches and attacks unfolded."

Cybersecurity analysts realize that every person in an organization represents a potential security risk. For example, a user might use a weak, easily guessed password to access the system; inadvertently open an e-mail containing a virus; or click a link that downloads damaging software known as malware. Cybersecurity analysts develop security standards and best practices for their organizations and then communicate them to the employees. They often provide security training to other employees and send out updates and bulletins to keep them informed about possible threats.

How Do You Become a Cybersecurity Analyst?

Education

Most cybersecurity analysts have earned a bachelor's degree in computer science, programming, engineering, or a related field. Some employers prefer candidates with specialized knowledge of cybersecurity, which may be obtained through a formal training program. Certain positions require work experience or advanced degrees, such as a Master of Business Administration in Information Systems.

The US armed forces also provides training in cybersecurity. For example, the Marine Corps offers training for cybersecurity technicians and information assurance technicians, while the Air Force trains for positions in cybersystems operations and cybersurety. Positions in the US Army—such as cryptologic network warfare specialist and military intelligence systems maintainer—also provide background for cybersecurity. Navy roles include information warfare, information technology, and computer science jobs.

Certification and Licensing

Cybersecurity analysts can gain certification through several professional organizations, such as EC-Council and ISACA, which offer programs for becoming a Certified Information Systems Auditor, Certified Information Security Manager, and Certified in Risk and Information Systems Control. Software vendors such as Microsoft and Cisco also offer certification for security professionals. The US Department of Homeland Security (DHS) offers certifications for cybersecurity analysts, including Introduction to Control Systems Cybersecurity and Intermediate Cybersecurity for Industrial Control Systems. "I can safely say that many industry certifications are of great value to the newcomer, novice and practitioner," writes Sid Vanderloot, an IT security academic with certifications from the DHS, EC-Council, and ISACA, in an article on LinkedIn. "Certification elevates one's knowledge to gain an understanding of both the theoretical and practical," Vanderloot told the author of this book in an interview.

Volunteer Work and Internships

An organization called I Am the Cavalry was formed in response to concerns over the impact of cybersecurity threats on public safety. All members of the organization are volunteers who offer their time and expertise free of charge to the medical, automotive, home electronics, and public infrastructure industries. Outside such organizations, few cybersecurity analysts have the opportunity to perform volunteer work, although some retired cybersecurity analysts may volunteer their time to nonprofit organizations.

Some companies, government offices, and computing research laboratories offer cybersecurity internships for undergraduates and graduate students. For example, the DHS offers the Secretary's Honors Program Cyber Student Volunteer Initiative for current college students pursuing a program of study in a cybersecurity-related field. Selected students learn about the DHS cybersecurity mission, complete hands-on cybersecurity work, and build technical experience in key areas such as digital forensics, network diagnostics, and incident response. The DHS also has a Cybersecurity Internship Program for undergraduate and graduate students. "Interns will have the opportunity to apply concepts, protocols and tools acquired through coursework in the real world by working side by side with experts in cybersecurity," states the DHS website. "Internships focus on mission areas such as identification and analysis of malicious code, forensics analysis, incident handling, intrusion detection and prevention, and software assurance."

Skills and Personality

Cybersecurity analysts need a broad understanding of IT, because hackers can attack any weakness in a networked system. "Remember, a career in cybersecurity means you're capable of everything a traditional IT person is capable of, and more. You're using all of your IT skills to push back the bad guys," writes Gewirtz.

Cybersecurity analysts also need to possess problem-solving skills that are similar to those of a detective so they can think like the adversary and anticipate what they might do. However, Gewirtz cautions about going too far: "Never, ever hack or crack. Stay away from the criminal and unethical stuff. While a few top hackers have romantic stories, they generally followed long jail sentences and solitary confinement. Few organizations hire ex-cons."

On the Job

Employers

About 26 percent of cybersecurity analysts work for computer systems design companies. Others work in finance, information, scientific and technical consulting, or enterprise management (firms that over-see and manage the business of other companies).

Working Conditions

Cybersecurity analysts work full time, indoors, often in a casual envi-ronment. According to the Bureau of Labor Statistics (BLS), about 25 percent of cybersecurity analysts work more than forty hours per week. Cybersecurity analysts remain on call after working hours so they can react to a security breach or emergency.

Earnings

According to a BLS nationwide survey, cybersecurity analysts earned a median annual wage of $90,120 in 2015—about 11 percent more than the median for computing professionals and about 2.5 times the median for all occupations. The top 10 percent of cybersecurity ana-lysts earned more than $143,770, while the lowest 10 percent earned less than $51,280.

Cybersecurity analysts report a high degree of job satisfaction, because they feel they are doing something useful. "For top talent, cybersecurity isn't about just a job and a paycheck," Jim Duffey, secre-tary of technology at the office of the governor of Virginia, told tech news site CIO.com. "It is about the hottest technology, deployed by honorable organizations, for a purpose that is inherently important."

Opportunities for Advancement

Experienced cybersecurity analysts can progress to the position of information security manager or chief information security officer. They also can go into business for themselves, providing private con-sulting to companies or working as contractors for a computing sys-tem design firm.

What Is the Future Outlook for Cybersecurity Analysts?

The job outlook for cybersecurity analysts is excellent. According to the BLS, employment is projected to grow by 18 percent nationwide through 2024, which is much faster than the average (7 percent) for all occupations and faster than the average (12 percent) of computing occupations. According to a study by Burning Glass Technologies, the demand for cybersecurity professionals grew more than 3.5 times faster than the demand for other IT jobs between 2009 and 2014 and more than 12 times faster than the demand for all other non-IT jobs. Staffing shortages are estimated between twenty thousand and forty thousand and are expected to continue for years to come.

Demand is driven by increasing efforts to fight cybercrime—not only in the private sector, but also in the public sector. Following the hacking of the IRS database in 2015, the federal government made plans to increase its use of cybersecurity analysts to protect the nation's critical IT systems. In addition the health care industry is expanding its use of electronic medical records, and this personal information must be protected from hackers.

According to the market research firm Gartner, the Internet of Things (IoT), a network of everyday objects connected to the Internet, will comprise 21 billion devices by 2020. Many of these devices will be in the home. Safeguarding the data collected by the IoT will be a foremost concern. Because of this and other security concerns, the BLS projects the employment of cybersecurity analysts to grow 36 percent in computer systems design and related services from 2014 to 2024.

Find Out More

Computer Forensics World
website: http://computerforensicsworld.com

Computer Forensics World is a community of professionals involved in the digital forensics industry. It is an open resource, free for all to access and use. Its website includes forums, posting areas, and educational materials on computer forensics and security.

Information Systems Security Association (ISSA)
9220 SW Barbur Blvd.
Portland, OR 97219
website: www.issa.org

The ISSA is a not-for-profit, international organization of information security professionals and practitioners. It provides educational forums, publications, and peer interaction opportunities that enhance the knowledge, skill, and professional growth of its members.

National Security Institute (NSI)
165 Main St., Suite 215
Medway, MA 02053
website: www.nsi.org

The NSI is dedicated to helping companies and governmental agencies understand threats to security. Its information services are used by top corporations to educate employees about risks to critical information from hackers, spies, and data thieves. The NSI's website contains articles and special reports about computer security.

SANS Institute
8120 Woodmont Ave., Suite 205
Bethesda, MD 20814
website: www.sans.org

The SANS Institute is a cooperative research and education organization that provides information security training and security certification. It develops, maintains, and makes available at no cost the largest collection of research documents about various aspects of information security.

Social Media Specialist

Every day hundreds of millions of Internet users visit social networking websites such as Facebook, Twitter, LinkedIn, Snapchat, Instagram, and YouTube. Businesses, nonprofit organizations, and individuals such as musicians, writers, and other artists post information, pictures, and videos on social networking websites to promote their brands and enter into a dialogue with customers and potential clients. Using social media in this way requires planning, strategy, and someone to do the work. That person is a social media specialist.

In many companies, social media activities are assigned as a part-time responsibility of an individual in the marketing department. Sometimes the responsibility is shared among several people. Internet-savvy companies hire a social media specialist to concentrate on just this aspect of an organization's marketing outreach and build a community around its brand and products.

At a Glance:
Social Media Specialist

Minimum Educational Requirements

Bachelor's degree or equivalent

Personal Qualities

Solid writing skills; creative; interested in social media; people oriented

Working Conditions

Indoors

Salary Range

About $27,000 to $59,000

Number of Jobs

As of 2014 about 240,700 (for all public relations specialists, including social media specialists)

Future Job Outlook

Growth rate of about 6 percent through 2024

50

A social media specialist might start the day by using social media tracking software such as Social Studio, Synthesio, Brandwatch, Digimind Social, or Brandango to identify trends, track competitors, and understand customer sentiment. Using tracking software, the specialist can generate a report of the amount of activity—views, likes, shares, and comments—the previous day's social media posts generated. "Monitoring the performance of the pages is crucial so I know which posts were good, which ones to avoid, and which ones need modification," Andrew Ike B. Waga, a social media specialist at StraightArrow Corporation, writes on his company's blog.

The specialist will scan comments made about posts and respond to selected ones to further engage with the customers, clients, and others. Anna Osgoodby, the social media director for a lifestyle PR firm called Media Maison, enjoys this personal interaction. "I love working on accounts that people freak out when we respond or retweet them on Twitter," Osgoodby told Business News Daily, a website for small businesses. "Having that brand connection is really important and I love when I get to make someone's day." Occasionally a comment will raise an issue the social media specialist is not qualified to answer or resolve. The specialist might bring the comment to the attention of the person of authority in the customer service, product management, or possibly the IT department.

While the social media specialist is responsible for producing the content posted online, the substance of the messaging typically originates in meetings with other stakeholders, such as marketing strategists, product managers, or even top management. The social media specialist usually meets with stakeholders to understand the messaging and then presents a plan to show the placement and timing of the social media posts. "I make a posting plan for each week," writes Waga.

> The plan includes all the posts and other content that will be published across all media platforms. Using knowledge gained from several webinars and certification classes, I follow the best practices per social media network, as each platform is different. Getting the right curated content is important; the goal of a social media specialist is to have each post radiate the company's brand and identity.

The social media specialist's plan must dovetail with and accentuate an organization's overall communication plan.

A social media specialist must be able to adapt to change and enjoy learning new things. "I like everything about my job. It is always changing. You get comfy with one platform and blink, and then something new comes along," Angie Robert, a senior communications manager of social media and digital content with Intuit, a company that develops financial and tax preparation software, said in an interview with the author. "It is cool to be a part of the customer journey and engage with them when they are thinking of our brand. Social media is different from many communications vehicles in that you can track it and quantify results."

How Do You Become a Social Media Specialist?

Education

Most large companies hiring a full-time social media specialist expect candidates to have a bachelor's degree in communications, marketing, or business. However, a candidate with an impressive social media presence—a large following on Twitter or Instagram, for example—a familiarity with social media tracking tools, and a strong writing portfolio likely can be hired regardless of educational background. "Anyone can build a Facebook page, but it doesn't mean it's successful," Gina Oliveri, senior consultant with executive staffing firm Bowdoin Group, told CIO.com.

> [Social media specialists] go deeper and rely on analytics to run good campaigns, tying it all back to ROI [return on investment]. They need to know not only how to run campaigns and ads, they need to know how it all ties back to ROI and how the business can generate revenue from it. You need to be a number-cruncher at some level—put on headphones and look at the data, then come back with intelligent insight so the business knows what to do next.

A social media specialist meets with other company employees to discuss the latest social media marketing strategy. These specialists use multiple platforms to enhance the company's image and identity.

Volunteer Work and Internships

Anyone aged thirteen and older can have social media accounts on Facebook, Twitter, Instagram, Pinterest, Tumblr, Reddit, Snapchat, and—with their parents' permission—YouTube. Those fourteen and older can add LinkedIn to the social media list. Many social media analysis tools are free online. As a result, almost anyone can volunteer to act as a social media specialist for an organization or self-employed individual. Since most organizations need to build their web presence, they often will accept a social media specialist to help. Volunteering is a great way to gain knowledge about the various social media platforms and gain experience building a social media presence that can be documented.

Skills and Personality

Social media platforms are designed for anyone to use, so social media specialists do not need special technical skills. However, basic Hypertext Markup Language (HTML) skills can prove helpful for blogging and for posting comments with embedded links to the company's or client's website. Good writing skills are essential. The social media specialist must be able to convey an idea in a limited number of words or characters, and the specialist's language reflects directly on the reputation of the company or client. "Social media is often the place where someone will first hear about the business, so every tweet or post needs to make the best impression on the audience," Becky Saunders, social media executive at Ultimate Asset, writes on her company's website. "Often it is the start of their journey with you. They'll see a tweet, they'll go to a blog, they share the blog, or better still they fill in a form and become a lead. Getting this journey perfect will really give you some job satisfaction."

A good sense of humor is helpful for creating posts that are so witty or entertaining that they are shared many times over. Some graphic design, video editing, and digital photo enhancement skills are helpful for creating memes—creative concepts, catchphrases, or pieces of media that spread from person to person via the Internet.

On the Job

Employers

Any organization, large or small, that has a web presence most likely is using social media to engage with its customers, increase awareness of its products or services, and drive traffic to its website. According to HubSpot, the real estate industry is responsible for more business-related social media posts than any other industry. More than 19 percent of business-related posts are about real estate. Marketing services is next with 14 percent, then software and tech with about 10 percent. Computer hardware, nonprofit and education, and the financial industry are each responsible for about 8 percent of social media posts.

Working Conditions

Social media specialists usually work indoors in a casual environment and keep regular hours. However, most can and often do work anywhere they have a smartphone, keeping up-to-date on social media posts and posting new content at any time, day or night. "Realize that the Internet doesn't turn off and that social media is a 24-7 job," Dave Amirault, director of marketing for the Snowbird resort in Utah, told MarketerGizmo. Because social media specialists can perform most of their duties on mobile devices, they often are allowed to telecommute one or more days a week.

Earnings

According to PayScale, the median salary of a social media specialist is $41,000 a year, ranging from a low of $27,000 to a high of $59,000 a year. Some companies provide bonuses of up to $5,000 for outstanding performance. Other firms offer profit sharing of up to $6,000 if personal and business targets are reached. Location has a big impact on the salaries of social media specialists. Specialists in San Francisco earn 37 percent more than the national average, according to PayScale. Social media specialists earn 26 percent more than the national average in Boston, 21 percent more in Seattle, and 15 percent more in Atlanta. Social media specialists in Austin earn about 13 percent less than the national average.

Although the median salary of social media specialists is about half that of all computing-related occupations, it is about 14 percent higher than the median for all occupations. Despite the moderate pay, PayScale reports that "job satisfaction is high and work is enjoyable for most social media specialists."

Opportunities for Advancement

Since social media marketing is still a new endeavor, there is no defined social media career path. Social media specialists usually follow one of two paths: They build on their content creation to become more deeply involved in digital communications, or they delve more deeply into the analytics side of their job and become strategists or data analysts. Either path can lead to management positions. For example, a social media specialist who enjoys content creation might advance to content manager, progress to head of content, then to head of digital communications, and finally to head of digital. A more analytical social media specialist might advance to social media manager, progress to head of social/paid media, then to head of digital communications, and finally to head of digital.

What Is the Future Outlook for Social Media Specialists?

According to a study by the University of New Orleans, the one-year job growth for social media specialists in 2013 was an amazing 42 percent. Marketing research firm Gartner found that executives at 98 percent of 339 large and extra-large companies in North America and the United Kingdom say online and offline marketing are merging. Fully 65 percent of the businesses surveyed ranked social media marketing on their list of top five priorities—the highest percentage of any of the top technology investments. Increased spending means increased jobs, since social media marketing requires people to post content and engage customers. The Bureau of Labor Statistics (BLS), which includes social media specialists among public relations specialists, forecasts growth of 6 percent through 2024, which was as fast as the average for all occupations.

Find Out More

Social Media Club
PO Box 14881
San Francisco, CA 94114
website: http://socialmediaclub.org

The Social Media Club's mission is to promote media literacy and standard technologies, encourage ethical behavior, and share best practices among social media professionals. The organization's website contains links to several club blogs and social media events, as well as general educational materials.

Social Media Professional Association
530 Lytton Ave.
Palo Alto, CA 94301
website: www.certificationinsocialmedia.com

The Social Media Professional Association is an organization that provides training, education, and certification in social media marketing. The website contains links to articles and research about social media in a marketing context.

Social Media Today
website: www.socialmediatoday.com

Social Media Today is an independent online community for professionals in public relations, marketing, advertising, and other disciplines that rely on social media. The website hosts lively debates about the tools, platforms, companies, and personalities that are revolutionizing the way information is consumed. Articles are contributed by professionals who work with social media.

Word of Mouth Marketing Association (WOMMA)
65 E. Wacker Place, Suite 500
Chicago, IL 60601
website: http://womma.org

WOMMA is the official trade association dedicated to word-of-mouth and social media marketing. The website contains information about best practices, regulations, and opportunities within digital media. Various online publications are available to nonmembers at no cost, as is WOMMA's industry blog.

Mobile App Developer

More than 2.5 billion people access the Internet via smartphones, a number expected to grow to 6.1 billion by 2020. In many parts of the world, more people connect to the Internet with smartphones than with computers. The applications that run on smartphones not only are downloaded from the Internet, but also often store and access data online. The people who develop applications, or apps, for smartphones are known as mobile app developers. Developing apps for smartphones is one of the fastest-growing areas of software development.

More than four million mobile apps were available as of June 2016—2.2 million for the Android platform and 2 million for Apple's iOS platform. "Mobile app development is a never ending technology field, because the smartphone has become a vital gadget for the people," programmer and blogger Carter Jack writes on Quora.com. "The

At a Glance:
Mobile App Developer

Minimum Educational Requirements
Bachelor's degree or equivalent

Personal Qualities
Creative problem solving; systematic; detail oriented

Certification and Licensing
Strongly preferred

Working Conditions
Indoors

Salary Range
About $57,000 to $154,000

Number of Jobs
As of 2014 about 718,000

Future Job Outlook
Growth rate of about 19 percent through 2024

increasing number of mobile applications shows that smartphone app development is the good choice for your career."

Mobile app developers write, test, and debug code for mobile applications. Usually these apps are new, but sometimes mobile developers migrate and adapt existing web applications to the leading mobile platforms. However, mobile apps are not just desktop apps formatted for small screens. The mobile web developer works closely with the user experience developer to make sure that mobile Internet users have the best possible experience when visiting a website. "The way people interact with a laptop or a desktop is different than the way they interact with a smart device," Hap Aziz, director of the Rasmussen College Schools of Technology and Design, told *Computerworld*. "People using a smart device don't think of themselves as 'computer users,' therefore you can't use the same conventions you'd use in developing desktop software. Drop-down menus and elaborate help screens just don't work on a smart device—it's more like working an ATM machine at the bank."

The tech team for payroll services company ADP learned this lesson the hard way when it began work on a mobile app. "We started out with a list of 100 features that we thought were awesome," Roberto Masiero, head of the innovation labs for ADP, told *Computerworld*. By the time they were done, they had reduced the number of features to twenty. "We learned that you have to drop completeness in the name of usefulness," said Masiero.

One of the best ways to prepare for a career in mobile app development is to observe human interactions and tasks through the lens of computing—a process Jeannette Wing, head of the Computer Science Department at Carnegie Mellon University, calls computational thinking. "At what point do you stop renting skis and buy yourself a pair?" writes Wing in *Communications of the ACM*. "That's online algorithms. Which line do you stand in at the supermarket?; that's performance modeling for multi-server systems. Why does your telephone still work during a power outage?; that's independence of failure and redundancy in design." By applying computing concepts to everyday life, would-be mobile app developers will find themselves asking, "How can I app that?" If the answer reveals something a computer can do better and faster than a human being, the mobile app developer may have found the basis for "the next big thing" in mobile apps.

How Do You Become a Mobile App Developer?

Education

Most employers seek mobile app developers who have at least a bachelor's degree in computer science, software engineering, mobile application development, mobile computing, or a related field. Some employers may prefer candidates to have a master's degree. Many employers want to see a portfolio of an applicant's software development projects, especially—but not limited to—mobile applications.

Since 90 percent of mobile apps are written for iOS or Android operating systems, employers prefer candidates with application development for these environments. Knowledge of one or more of the common mobile app programming languages—Objective-C, C++, C#, or Java—is highly desirable. Depending on the type of apps a company develops, it might require experience with game programming, user interface (UI) design, or mobile media marketing. A mobile app developer sometimes needs skills related to the industry in which they wish to work. For example, a developer working for the health care industry should have a basic understanding of the health care system so that the app will address real-world needs.

Certification and Licensing

Most software developers see certification as a way to quickly determine a candidate's fluency in the skills that meet business demands and expectations. Certifications in mobile app development are available from vendors such as Apple and Microsoft as well as from non-vendors such as the nonprofit organization Mobile Development Institute (MDI). MDI offers three entry-level MDI Certified Developer certifications for Apple iOS, Google Android, and BlackBerry. To qualify for an MDI certification exam, candidates must have published at least one app on one of the platforms. Online education provider Learning Tree offers a program to become a Certified Specialist in Android Application Development, iOS Application Development, and Multi-Device Mobile Application Development. The Microsoft Technology Associate program offers Mobile Development Fundamentals certification that tests a candidate's ability to work with Windows Phone mobile devices, networked data, and data stores; evaluate mobile programming code in XNA, Visual Basic, .NET, HTML5, XAML, and C#; and develop mobile apps.

Volunteer Work and Internships

Apps are an excellent way for a nonprofit organization to build relationships with mobile device users. As a result, many nonprofit organizations are seeking mobile app developers who will devote their time to creating apps that promote the organization's goals. For example, ServiceSpace, a nonprofit organization that promotes volunteerism, advertised on its website: "ServiceSpace is going mobile! We are looking to design mobile apps that help foster habits around the values of kindness, generosity, and service."

With a nationwide shortage of mobile app developers, it is no surprise that companies are seeking to train interns who can then build or update apps. For example, EF (Education First), which creates learning experiences for travelers, advertised to students and recent graduates on Indeed.com: "As an intern for Go Ahead Tours you will work on a small autonomous and agile team. Your work will make it to the AppStore and will be seen by tens of thousands of our customers." Such internships often lead to permanent positions as mobile app developers.

Skills and Personality

Mobile app developers must be creative problem solvers yet highly disciplined and methodical in the creation of software code. They must be inspired by elegant mobile apps and aspire to create them. To make this a reality, they must understand one or more of the four major mobile platforms: Android, iOS (Apple), RIM (Blackberry), and Windows Mobile. They also need to know one or more of the related core languages: Java, Objective-C, Java, C++, and C#. "Businesses

A mobile app developer works on preliminary design ideas for a new smartphone app. Their work includes designing, writing, testing, and debugging code for mobile applications.

typically develop mobile applications for multiple platforms at once, to maximize market penetration and return on investment—so the more mobile development platforms you learn and master, the more sought-after you become as a professional mobile application developer," Mark Lassoff, an instructor in web and mobile application development, writes on the ITCareerFinder website.

Mobile app developers often meet with clients or stakeholders and work in teams with UX designers, other app developers, and back end developers, so they must have excellent interpersonal skills. They also need strong math skills. Although they rarely write content for their apps, mobile app developers need good writing skills so they can document their work.

On the Job

Employers

The gaming industry dominates the mobile app market; 49 percent of all downloaded apps are games. However, the other 51 percent of downloaded apps come from a wide range of industries. Thousands of companies realize the value of mobile apps for promoting their businesses. This includes online businesses, but it also includes non-Internet, "brick-and-mortar" businesses. For example, restaurant chain Krispy Kreme offers a free app for both Apple and Android phones that tells customers when hot doughnuts are expected to come off the line. The app, called Hot Light, even sends push notifications when the Hot Light is on at a user's nearest Krispy Kreme location. Many of these apps are developed within the organizations, but the majority are developed by computing service companies.

A mobile app developer does not need to work for any company—large or small—to submit their app for distribution. For example, Anvitha Vijay, age nine, developed an iPad/iPhone app about animals called Smartkins Animals. The app was accepted for distribution through the Apple Store, and Vijay became the youngest developer to attend Apple's Worldwide Developers Conference in June 2016. Similarly, when he was fourteen, Robert Nay created the gaming app Bubble Ball. Released in December 2010, Bubble Ball has been downloaded more than 16 million times, and Nay is one of America's youngest millionaires.

Working Conditions

Mobile app developers work indoors, usually in a casual environment. Most work full time and often work long hours to meet deadlines. Because application coding and testing normally can be performed on laptop computers, mobile app developers can work virtually anywhere. As a result, many telecommute at least a few days a month.

Earnings

According to the Bureau of Labor Statistics (BLS), the median annual wage for mobile app developers was $98,260 in May 2015. The lowest 10 percent earned less than $57,340, and the highest 10 percent earned more than $153,710. Indeed.com places the median annual salary for mobile app developers a little higher, at $104,000 a year, with lead iOS developers earning $117,000 a year, regular iOS developers earning $91,000 a year, and general mobile app developers earning $81,000 a year.

Opportunities for Advancement

Most companies provide for advancement within the field of software development, from junior developer, to developer, to senior or lead developer. Mobile app developers who learn back end programming can become full stack developers. Experienced mobile app developers can become software architects, responsible for complex software development projects that often include connecting an app to databases and other systems, such as management systems. App developers with outstanding communications and conceptualization skills can become a UX designer. Those with managerial and leadership skills may move into project management or department management roles.

What Is the Future Outlook for Mobile App Developers?

The BLS forecasts that the job market for mobile app developers is expected to increase by 19 percent through 2024, creating more than 135,000 new positions. This growth is greater than the growth for all software developers (17 percent), systems software developers (13 percent), and all computing occupations (12 percent). The vast majority of job opportunities will be in Android and iOS app development, as these platforms represent more than 90 percent of all mobile devices used in the United States.

Find Out More

Application Developers Alliance
1015 Seventh St. NW
Washington, DC 20001
website: www.appdevelopersalliance.org

Founded in 2012 the Application Developers Alliance supports developers as an essential workforce through education, advocacy, and thought leadership. It also works to raise the profile of developers among policy makers, the business community, and the media. The alliance's website includes white papers, research, infographics, and best practice guides.

App QualityAlliance (AQuA)
website: www. appqualityalliance.org

AQuA is a global association focused on helping the industry continually improve and promote mobile app quality across all platforms. AQuA acts as a referral and endorsement body, accrediting the quality of developers and their apps. The organization offers developers tools to test their apps for common errors, accessibility, and network performance.

Association of Software Professionals (ASP)
PO Box 1522
Martinsville, IN 46151
website: http://asp-software.org

The ASP is a professional trade association of software developers who are creating desktop and laptop programs, Software as a Service applications, cloud computing, and mobile apps. The association publishes a monthly newsletter and maintains a library of twenty-five years of newsletter articles and more than five years of member-to-member discussions.

Penetration Tester

What Does a Penetration Tester Do?

A penetration tester—pentester for short—is a network security specialist who tries to break into or find possible weaknesses in computer networks, systems, and software. Because pentesters use many of the same tools and techniques that malicious hackers use to breach security, they are sometimes described as "white hat" hackers or "ethical hackers." In fact, Certified Ethical Hacking is a security certification offered by EC-Council, a member-supported professional certification organization, and many people refer to themselves as ethical hackers on LinkedIn and other career websites. "I've been hacking full-time for the last five years and it's really one of the most interesting and challenging jobs anyone can have," Ben Miller, a pentester at Parameter Security, told Life Hack.com. "It's also incredibly rewarding, because I know I'm helping to protect companies and institutions from malicious hackers who would otherwise have nothing to stop them from breaking in."

During a typical day, a pentester will run a number of tests against web-based applications, networks, and other types of computer systems and then create assessment reports about what they have found. Pentesters often run standard tests using commercially developed security software, but they often devise their own tests based on their knowledge of hardware, software, network protocols, and human nature. Creating new tests to probe security requires creativity and imagination combined with a high level of technical know-how. "To be honest, there is a thrill in knowing that what I do would be illegal except for a legal document that says I'm allowed to do it without getting in trouble," says Miller. "One of my favorite compliments from my former place of work was, 'You think like a criminal!' They didn't mean it as a compliment."

Unlike security analysts, pentesters do not simply scan networks, looking for vulnerabilities. Once they find an opening, they must identify what the practical consequences of an intrusion might be for that institution. They probe deeper into the system as a hacker would, looking for ways to steal data, perform illegal funds transfers, or interfere with operations. "You have to be creative to see the full potential of a security flaw and to put all the pieces together to figure out how a criminal would pull off a data or financial heist," says Miller.

Pentesters then must demonstrate the business impact of the security flaws to their clients or their organization's management. "Successful penetration testers don't just throw a bunch of hacks against an organization and regurgitate the output of their tools," Ed Skoudis, the founder of cybersecurity firm Counter Hack, writes on the SANS Institute website. "Instead, they need to understand how these tools work in depth, and conduct their test in a careful, professional manner."

Not all of the techniques a pentester uses are high tech. Using a technique called social engineering testing, pentesters employ "trusted authority" disguises, such as fire inspectors, air-conditioning repair personnel, or pest control professionals to gain access to a building and use a computer. Sometimes pentesters will impersonate employees, such as IT help desk, new hires, or auditors to contact employees by phone or e-mail to gain a password or other restricted information. Often a pentester will mine social networking sites, search engines, blogs, and other readily available sources to gain the trust of people at the targeted organization. "I absolutely love my job," Jason Haddix, director of technical operations at Bugcrowd, writes on the LinkedIn website. "I am passionate about information security. Not only is security my career focus but it's my hobby."

Hackers rarely gain access to a system soon after targeting it. It can take months to learn about people within the organization who might be tricked or coerced into allowing the hacker in (a process known as social engineering). It also takes time to probe the security system to find a weakness that can be exploited. Pentesters cannot spend that much time on a test. Instead, they use sophisticated tools to look for vulnerabilities such as software programs never updated with security patches; default passwords such as "admin" or "1234" still being used; open ports, such as the ones set aside for the now mostly obsolete communications protocol Telnet; and older, less secure hardware connected to the network. For example, TrapX, a cybersecurity firm, found three cases in which hackers gained access to sensitive hospital records through unsecured medical devices such as X-ray machines and blood gas analyzers. Often installed a decade or more ago, such machines are connected to the hospital's internal network, but run older, easily exploited operating systems or are not updated with sophisticated virus or malware protection.

Pentesters are responsible for identifying problems, not for fixing them. They must communicate the results of their testing in easily understandable reports that describe not only the technical issues, but also the real-world ramifications of not fixing them. "Much of my time is spent probing or scanning networks, looking for vulnerabilities, etc., but just as much time is spent communicating with the client and documenting what I've done in a written report," says Miller. "I tell hacker students and new employees, 'You will write more reports as a hacker than you ever did at school!' The deliverable report is the one piece of the engagement that a client will keep and be able to mull over long after the 'warm fuzzies' from your personal care have faded. It needs to be just as good."

How Do You Become a Penetration Tester?

Education

A bachelor's degree in information technology or a cybersecurity-related field is commonly required by employers. Relevant certifications are often preferred. Experience can be substituted for education, especially when a candidate can demonstrate a working knowledge of hacking tools such Metasploit or Burp Suite or competing in "white hat" hacking contests. "In penetration testing, having a lack of schooling and higher education isn't necessarily a hindrance if you have some skill," writes pentester Lawrence Munro on the PenTesticles .com blog. "However, you will likely need to prove this to a greater extent than perhaps a graduate would." One way to do that is by earning bug bounties, which are payments made to ethical hackers who find a flaw or successfully penetrate a system. Munro adds that this is "a great way to prove your prowess, with sites such as Bugcrowd paying sizeable winnings to the best bug hunters."

Certification and Licensing

Many security-oriented organizations such as EC-Council and ISACA offer pentesting certificates such as Certified Ethical Hacker, Certified Penetration Tester, Certified Computer Forensics Examiner, and Certified Reverse Engineering Analyst. These certifications are especially helpful because they show the certificate holder not only understands the technology of pentesting, but also has learned the ethics of the practice.

Volunteer Work and Internships

Because pentesters probe and often breach a company's security system, gaining access to sensitive data, organizations usually do not seek volunteer pentesters. However, many companies as well as the US Department of Homeland Security (DHS) offer internships to undergraduate and graduate students interested in ethical hacking. For example, the Office of Intelligence and Analysis (I&A), part of DHS, offers an internship program for undergraduate and graduate students looking to begin a career in homeland security and intelligence. I&A offers internships in the areas of Intelligence Analysis, Intelligence Operations, Management/Support, Information Technology, and Policy. Such internships are an excellent way for a student or a recent graduate to become familiar with the specialized and often expensive software that both "black hat" and "white hat" hackers use.

Skills and Personality

Pentesters need specialized knowledge about a few things, such as bypassing software controls, password attacks, and other "black hat" practices. They also need general knowledge about the systems that hackers target: enterprise infrastructure, network architecture, system administration, database administration, and software development.

Problem solving, persistence, and good communication skills are all required for penetration testing. Pentesters are driven by intellectual curiosity and love a challenge. "We need more people who enjoy the puzzles, breaking things, fixing things, and the communication with people and the awesome experiences," says Miller.

On the Job

Employers

Every organization in both the public and private sectors has something to lose if they are hacked, and they often use pentesting to find their vulnerabilities. However, government offices such as the Internal Revenue Service, the Social Security Administration, and the Department of Health and Human Services possess sensitive information about citizens that must be kept confidential. Other government agencies, including the Defense Department and State Department, also must protect against hackers. As a result, the DHS trains and employs pentesters. The financial industry is a target of hackers because of the vast amounts of money it handles. As a result, the Payment Card Industry Data Security Standard requires penetration testing as part of regularly scheduled security audits and after changes to computing systems.

Working Conditions

Pentesters work indoors in a casual environment. Most pentesters who work as part of an IT team work normal, eight-hour days; those who work for a consulting firm might work ten-hour days while conducting a penetration test of a company. Sometimes pentesters are called in to help a company recover from a security breach. In such cases, the pentesters will work extremely long hours. "That's when you're in crisis mode and you can easily pull a few all-nighters trying to stop the attack from progressing, control the damage, and figure out how to get the company back on track," writes Miller.

Earnings

SilverBull, a technology recruitment company, reports that the median salary for pentesters is $124,000 a year. SilverBull estimates that the lowest 10 percent earns about $86,000 and the top 10 percent earns about $163,000. PayScale is not as generous in its estimate, however. It places the median salary of a pentester at about $78,000, with a range from $44,000 at the lower end to $124,000 at the higher end. The PayScale figure includes potential for approximately $14,000 each from bonuses and profit sharing. Indeed.com lands between the other two estimates, pegging the median salary of a pentester at $97,000.

Opportunities for Advancement

Some pentesters further specialize into areas such as software security for mobile and web apps; industrial control systems, such as those used in utilities and manufacturing plants; or social engineering. An experienced pentester with excellent people and organizational skills might lead a team of pentesters or be promoted to director of security or even chief information security officer of a company. A pentester who works for a software company could become a lead application security engineer or architect. Pentesters can use their knowledge of how to break into a system to become computer forensics analysts, investigating what happened during a security breach.

What Is the Future Outlook for Penetration Testers?

InfoSec Institute, an information security training company, rates the future job outlook of a penetration tester as "a solid B+." The company's website states, "As technology becomes a bigger part of more individual industries, the demand for penetration testers grows. However, because it's such a specialized job, you'll often have a steady amount of competition for job openings specific to penetration testing, especially at the entry level before you have work experience." The Bureau of Labor Statistics (BLS) does not give statistics for pentesters, but it forecasts that the entire field of cybersecurity will grow by 18 percent over the next ten years.

Find Out More

EC-Council
101C Sun Ave. NE
Albuquerque, NM 87109
website: www.eccouncil.org

EC-Council is a leading IT and e-business certification awarding body and the creator of the world-famous Certified Ethical Hacker, Computer Hacking Forensics Investigator, and EC-Council Certified Security Analyst/License Penetration Tester programs. The organization sponsors events such as TakeDownCon, a forum focusing on the latest vulnerabilities, the most potent exploits, and the current security threats.

Ethical Hacker Network
1520 Heidorn Ave.
Westchester, IL 60154
website: www.ethicalhacker.net

The Ethical Hacker Network is a free online magazine for security professionals. It provides articles designed to help pentesters learn what new things hackers are doing so they can secure their systems from attacks. The website offers discussion forums, lists of certification programs, and a calendar of upcoming events for ethical hackers.

SANS Institute
8120 Woodmont Ave., Suite 205
Bethesda, MD 20814
website: www.sans.org

Established in 1989 the SANS Institute is a cooperative research and education organization that provides information security training and security certification. It develops, maintains, and makes available at no cost the largest collection of research documents about various aspects of information security. Each year, SANS holds a Pen Test Hackfest Summit & Training event that includes six days of hands-on, immersion-style pentest training.

Interview with a Search Engine Optimization Manager

Mandy Ison is a senior search engine optimization manager for TurboTax in San Diego, California. She has worked in SEO for nine years. She answered questions about her career by e-mail.

Q: Why did you become a search engine optimization manager?

A: In the late 1990s, the Internet was just exploding, and I became fascinated with how to build websites. I taught myself HTML and PHP coding, starting small before moving on to build larger websites with shopping carts and photo galleries.

However, I often found that after launching a website, it was hard to find it in the search engines. After all that hard work, and no traffic? I scoured online resources and learned how to optimize a website to rank at the top of the search engine results. This became a skill I improved as new search engines emerged, like the all-important Google, and the advent of much more sophisticated SEO techniques.

After graduating college, my first full-time position was as an SEO specialist which, ironically, had little to do with my English degree, except for the strong writing skills. I have since built a career that has expanded beyond simple search engine optimization for websites to owning the end-to-end SEO strategy for a major brand, like TurboTax. I feel very lucky to be in a position to not only love what I do, but to also have a significant impact on the success of my employer's business.

Q: Can you describe your typical workday?

A: My typical workday starts with a cup of coffee! It then runs the gamut from SEO strategic planning to execution, as well as working on projects in collaboration with different business units. For strategic planning, this includes creating and finalizing the SEO plan for each year. As the SEO strategy is finalized, there are multiple parallel paths initiated to execute on parts of the plan that have a long lead time, those that must be started immediately in order to get a specific project completed by the next year.

Throughout a typical day, there may be meetings with internal stakeholders for specific business initiatives; calls with important agency partners who help execute parts of the SEO strategy; accessing dashboards and understanding what is driving SEO performance for the day, week, month, or year; creating and presenting PowerPoint presentations to teams and leaders; editing and approving content such as articles, videos, and slideshows; coordinating launches with other channels such as Paid Search and Offline advertising (TV); and much more. As a people manager, I also set aside time to meet 1:1 with my team, provide support, feedback, and help with project prioritization.

At the end of the day, there's a lot of time dedicated to answering e-mails, attending meetings, and jumping on calls!

Q: What do you like most and least about your job?

A: What I love most about search engine optimization is the fact that it's an ever-evolving field that constantly challenges me to be better. Search engines update their ranking algorithms frequently to more effectively remove spam and improve the relevancy of their results. While this is great for the end user, this also makes the job of an SEO harder and has led to search engine optimization expanding beyond the basics—for example, social media and mobile optimization.

What I like least is when leaders must be convinced of the value of SEO, or seek instant results, which has been an issue in past jobs. SEO is a long game. Improving a website's rankings take a lot of time, usually months to years. It's not on or off, it must be executed effectively year-round. When expectations are unrealistic or skeptical, getting the support you need to get projects done can be nearly impossible. I recommend working for companies or clients that already believe in the value of SEO so that this is one hurdle you don't have to overcome in order to make progress.

Q: What personal qualities do you find most valuable for this type of work?

A: I enjoy collaboration, and that's a big plus when you're working across teams with diverse skills: web architects, writers, designers, and more. Communicating clearly and effectively is critical to SEO success and for any job at a large business. A strong analytical mind-set is also vital. I enjoy numbers, statistics, and probabilities. Each SEO initiative is like a small social experiment, and the results will either prove or disprove your hypothesis. I love analyzing results and understanding what's behind them. It's a blend of numbers and human behavior.

Q: What advice do you have for students who might be interested in this career?

A: Start with finding a local agency or online company that offers SEO services and begin at an entry-level job to learn the ropes. Most entry-level SEO positions start with link building or keyword research, which is a solid foundation for building an SEO career. Sign up for top news sites about SEO and the search engines, like Search EngineLand.com. Read the beginner's guide to SEO on Moz.com and check out Bruce Clay's SEO tutorials. Subscribe to Google's *Webmaster* blog to learn from their announcements and updates, as well as their video resources on the Google Webmaster YouTube channel.

Other Jobs in Internet Technology

3-D animator
Blogger
Computing research scientist
Data modeler
Digital communications
  manager
Digital marketer
Help desk technician
Information security analyst
Instructional designer
  (e-learning)
Interactive producer
Internet marketer
Internet technology teacher
Multimedia animator
Multimedia artist
Network administrator

Network architect
Network support specialist
Pay per click manager
SEO analyst
SEO strategist
Social media manager
Telecommunication specialist
User interface designer
Video game designer
Web content writer
Web designer
Webmaster
Website administrator
Wi-Fi installer
Wireless communications
  technician

Editor's Note: The US Department of Labor's Bureau of Labor Statistics provides information about hundreds of occupations. The agency's *Occupational Outlook Handbook* describes what these jobs entail, the work environment, education and skill requirements, pay, future outlook, and more. The *Occupational Outlook Handbook* may be accessed online at www.bls.gov/ooh.

Index

Note: Boldface page numbers indicate illustrations

algorithms, 28
Amirault, Dave, 55
Apple, 15, 60
Application Developers Alliance, 64
App QualityAlliance (AQuA), 65
apps, number of, 58
Association for Computing Machinery
    (ACM), 40
Association of Software Professionals (ASP),
    65
Axure (software), 15
Aziz, Hap, 59

back end web developers, 18, 19
Big Data analytics, 7, 9
Boileau, Troy, 30
bots, 27
Brazen, 16
Brisco, Rosemary, 11
Bubble Ball app, 63
Burning Glass Technologies, 48
Business News Daily (website), 51

California State University, Fullerton, 14
Cascading Style Sheets (CSS), described, 19
certification and licensing
    of cybersecurity analysts, 42, 45
    of database administrators, 34, 36–37
    of mobile app developers, 58, 60–61
    of penetration testers, 66, 68, 69
    of search engine optimization managers, 26
    of user experience designers, 13–14
    of web developers, 18, 21–22
Certification Magazine (online publication), 35
Certified Ethical Hacking certification, 66
CNN Money, 16, 39
Communications of the ACM (magazine), 59
Computer Forensics World (website), 48
Computerworld (magazine), 59
content management systems, described, 19
cybersecurity analysts
    advancement opportunities for, 47
    basic facts about, 42
    certification and licensing of, 45
    earnings for, 47
    education requirements for, 44–45
    employers of, 46–47
    information sources for, 48–49

job description of, 42–44, 47
job outlook for, 47–48
personal skills and qualities of, 46
volunteer work and internships for, 45–46
cybersecurity jobs, job outlook for, 6

Data Administration Newsletter (TDAN.
    com), 40
database, defined, 34
database administrators (DBAs)
    advancement opportunities for, 39
    basic facts about, 34
    certification and licensing of, 36–37
    earnings and benefits for, 39
    education requirements for, 36
    employers of, 38
    information sources for, 40–41
    job description of, 34–36, 38–39
    job outlook for, 39
    personal skills and qualities of, 37–38
    volunteer work and internships for, 37
database management systems, types of, 38
data encryption software, 43
Data Management Association (DAMA)
    International, 40
digital marketing, 7, 9
Duffey, Jim, 47

earnings and benefits
    for cybersecurity analysts, 42, 47
    for database administrators, 34, 39
    for Internet technology careers, 8
    for mobile app developers, 58, 63
    for penetration testers, 66, 71
    for search engine optimization managers,
        26, 31
    for social media specialists, 50, 55
    for user experience designers, 10, 15–16
    for web developers, 18, 24
EC-Council
    about, 72
    and certification of cybersecurity analysts,
        45
    and certification of penetration testers,
        66, 69
education requirements
    for cybersecurity analysts, 42, 44–45
    for database administrators, 34, 36
    for Internet technology careers, 8
    for mobile app developers, 58, 60

for penetration testers, 66, 68–69
for search engine optimization managers, 26, 28–29
for social media specialists, 50, 52
for user experience designers, 10, 12–13
for web developers, 18, 21
EF (Education First), 61
Ethical Hacker Network, 72
ethical hackers. *See* penetration testers (pentesters)

Facebook, as employer, 15, 20
Farrell, Susan, 12–13
Favreau, Annie, 16
firewalls, described, 43
freelance opportunities, 23, 38
front end web developers, 18–19, 21
full stack developers, 18, 20–21

Gartner, 48, 56
General Assembly certification, 14
Gewirtz, David, 44, 46

hackers/hacking events, 35, 42–43
See also penetration testers (pentesters)
Haddix, Jason, 67
Host intrusion detection system (HIDS), 43
Hot Light (Krispy Kreme app), 63
HubSpot, 54
Human Factors and Ergonomics Society, 16
Hypertext Markup Language (HTML)
certification, 22
described, 19
knowledge of
mobile app and, 60, 61
search engine optimization managers and, 27, 29, 73
social media specialists and, 54

I Am the Cavalry (organization), 45
inbound links, 26, 27
Indeed.com, 61, 63, 71
Information Systems Security Association (ISSA), 48–49
information technology sector, current employment, 6
InfoSec Institute, 71–72
in-house search engine optimization managers, 30
Intelligent Personal Assistants (IPAs), 7
Interaction Design Association (IxDA), 17
International DB2 Users Group (IDUG), 40
International Webmasters Association (IWA), 24–25
Internet, number of devices connected to, 6
Internet of Things (IoT)
cybersecurity for, 48
number of devices connected to, 6
Web 3.0 and, 7

internships. *See* volunteer work and internships
ISACA, 45, 69
Ison, Mandy, 73–75

Jack, Carter, 58–59
JavaScript, described, 19
job descriptions
of cybersecurity analysts, 42–44, 47
of database administrators, 34–36, 38–39
of mobile app developers, 58, 59–60, 62, 63
of penetration testers, 66–68, 70–71
of search engine optimization managers, 26–28, 31, 74
of social media specialists, 50, 51–52, 55
of user experience designers, 10–12, 13, 15, 62
of web developers, 18–21, 23
job outlook
for computing-related and all cybersecurity jobs, 6
for cybersecurity analysts, 42, 47–48
for database administrators, 34, 39
for mobile app developers, 58, 64
for penetration testers, 66, 71–72
for search engine optimization managers, 26, 31–32
for skilled IT professionals, 9
for social media specialists, 50, 56
for user experience designers, 10, 16
for web developers, 6, 18, 24
Joyce, Julie, 28
Juniper Research, 6

Kalt, David, 21
keywords, 26, 27, 28

Lamprecht, Emil, 10, 11
Lassoff, Mark, 62
Learning Tree, 61
Lee, Shannon, 22

Magain, Matthew, 11, 12, 14
Manning, Doug, 19
Masiero, Roberto, 59
Microsoft Corporation, 22, 60, 61
Miller, Ben, on penetration testers
and being in crisis mode, 70–71
and job description, 68
and personal skills and qualities, 67, 70
and rewards of career, 66, 67
mobile app developers
advancement opportunities for, 64
basic facts about, 58
certification and licensing of, 60–61
earnings for, 63
education requirements for, 60
employers of, 62–63
information sources for, 64–65

job description of, 59–60, 62, 63
job outlook for, 64
personal skills and qualities of, 61–62
volunteer work and internships for, 61
mobile apps, number of, 58
Mobile Development Institute (MDI)
    certification, 60
Mockups.me (software), 15
Morris, Matthew, 35
Moz, 32
Munro, Lawrence, 69

National Center for Women & Information
    Technology, 32
National Security Institute (NSI), 49
Nay, Robert, 63
network intrusion detection systems,
    described, 43
Nielsen, Jakob, 12–13
Nielsen Norman Group (NNG), 12–14

Occupational Outlook Handbook (Bureau of
    Labor Statistics), 76
Office of Intelligence and Analysis (I&A), 69
off-page optimization, 27
Oliveri, Gina, 52
on-page optimization, 27
Oracle, 36–37
Orin, Andy, 21
Osgoodby, Anna, 51

Payment Card Industry Data Security
    Standard, 70
PayScale, 55, 71
penetration testers (pentesters)
    advancement opportunities for , 71
    basic facts about, 66
    certification and licensing of, 68, 69
    earnings for, 71
    education requirements for, 68–69
    employers of, 70
    information sources for, 72
    job description of, 66–68, 70–71
    job outlook for, 71–72
    personal skills and qualities of, 67, 70
    volunteer work and internships for, 69
penetration testing, described, 44
PenTesticles.com, 69
personal identification systems, described, 43
personal skills and qualities
    of cybersecurity analysts, 42, 46
    of database administrators, 34, 37–38
    of mobile app developers, 58, 61–62
    of penetration testers, 66, 67, 70
    of search engine optimization managers,
        26, 29–30, 75
    of social media specialists, 50, 54
    of user experience designers, 10, 14–15
    of web developers, 18, 21, 22

personas, described, 12
Petrovic, Dan, 28
Pixate, 15

Quesenbery, Whitney, 14–15
Quora.com, 58–59

Radicati Group, 7
Robert, Angie, 52
Robert Half Technology, 9

SANS Institute
    about, 49, 72
    penetration testers, 67
Saunders, Becky, 54
SearchDataManagement, 40
Search Engine Land, 32
search engine optimization (SEO) managers
    advancement opportunities for, 31
    basic facts about, 26
    earnings for, 31
    education requirements for, 28–29
    employers of, 30
    information sources for, 32–33
    job description of, 26–28, 31, 74
    job outlook for, 31–32
    personal skills and qualities of, 29–30, 75
    volunteer work and internships for, 29
search engine robots (bots), 27
self-employment opportunities, 23, 38
SEMPO, 33
ServiceMax, 14
ServiceSpace, 61
SilverBull, 71
Skoudis, Ed, 67
Smartkins Animals app, 63
smartphones, and number connected to
    Internet, 6, 58
Smith, Loretta Mahon, 36
social engineering testing, described, 67
Social Media Club, 56
Social Media Professional Association, 57
social media specialists
    advancement opportunities for, 55–56
    basic facts about, 50
    earnings for, 55
    education requirements for, 52
    employers of, 50, 54
    information sources for, 56–57
    job description of, 50, 51–52, 55
    job outlook for, 56
    personal skills and qualities of, 54
    volunteer work and internships for, 52
Social Media Today (website), 57
social networking
    marketing and, 7, 9
    and number of users (2016), 7
software development professionals, shortage
    of, 9

Special Interest Group on Computer-Human
Interaction (SIGCHI), 17
Stasiuk, Colin, 36
storyboards, described, 12
Structured Query Language (SQL), 37–38

Technology Councils of North America, 9
Thomas, Michael, 19
tracking software, 51
TrapX, 68

UK Council of Professors and Heads of
Computing, 9
University of Baltimore, 14
University of California, San Diego,
Extension, 14
University of New Orleans, 56
US Armed Forces, 45
US Bureau of Labor Statistics (BLS)
on current employment in information
technology sector, 6
on earnings
for database administrators, 39
and median for computer and
information technology occupations
(2015), 9
for mobile app developers, 63
for web developers, 24
on employers of database administrators, 38
on employers of web developers, 23
on hours worked by cybersecurity analysts,
47
on increase in science and engineering jobs
in computing (2004–2014), 6
on job outlook
for all computing-related jobs, 6
for cybersecurity analysts, 47–48
for cybersecurity field, 6, 72
for database administrators, 39
for mobile app developers, 64
for social media specialists, 56
for web developers, 6, 24
on types of Internet technology jobs, 76
US Department of Homeland Security (DHS)
cybersecurity analysts certification, 45
cybersecurity analyst volunteer and
internship programs with, 46
penetration tester internship programs
with, 69
as penetration tester trainer and employer,
70
user experience (UX) designers
basic facts about, 10
certification of, 13–14
earnings for, 15–16
education requirements for, 12–13
employers of, 15
information sources for, 16–17

job description of, 10–12, 13, 15, 62
job outlook for, 16
personal skills and qualities of, 14–15
volunteer work and internships for, 14
User Experience Professionals Association
(UXPA)
about, 17
on earnings of UX designers, 15
on educational level of UX designers, 12
on employers of UX designers, 15
user interface (UI) designers, 10
user testing, described, 11, 12
US Internal Revenue Service (IRS), 43
U.S. News & World Report (magazine), 36
UXPin, 15

Vanderloot, Sid, 45
Vijay, Anvitha, 63
volunteer work and internships
for cybersecurity analysts, 45–46
for database administrators, 37
for mobile app developers, 61
for penetration testers, 69
for search engine optimization managers,
29
for social media specialists, 52
for user experience designers, 14
for web developers, 22

Waga, Andrew Ike B., 51
Wales, Michael, 20
web designers, 10
web developers
advancement opportunities for, 24
basic facts about, 18
certification and licensing of, 21–22
earnings for, 24
education requirements for, 21
employers of, 20, 23
information sources for, 24–25
job description of, 18–21, 23
job outlook for, 6, 24
personal skills and qualities of, 21, 22
types of, 18–21
user experience designers and, 10, 11, 12
volunteer work and internships for, 22
Weber, Gerald, 32
Webgrrls International, 24–25
WebProfessionals.org, 24–25
Web 3.0, 7
white hat hackers. *See* penetration testers
(pentesters)
Wigal, Nancy E., 30
Wing, Jeannette, 59
wireframes, 11, 15
Word of Mouth Marketing Association
(WOMMA), 57
World Wide Web, 18